AMIE RYAN

MARILYN: Loved By You

AMIE RYAN

ALSO BY AMIE RYAN

Green Shoes Mean I Love You
Starfish On Thursday

Copyright © 2016 Amie Ryan

For information, JavaTown Press, 1425 Broadway #23499, Seattle, WA. 98122

A previous edition of this book was published in 2015 by Amie Ryan.

ISBN: 1511531827
ISBN-13: 978-1511531825

Library of Congress Control Number 2016909777

www.amieryan.com

Cover design by Dane Egenes

6

ACKNOWLEDGMENTS

I wish to thank: Shelly Petersen for her friendship and support, K.L. Dimago and tt Thomas for helping to spread the word about this book on Pinterest, Dane Egenes for designing the beautiful cover, and Nick for his insight and for being wonderful. I love you Nick. xoxo.

TO NICK

"I used to say to myself, 'What the devil have you got to be so proud about, Marilyn Monroe?' And I'd answer: 'Everything, everything,' and I'd walk slowly and turn my head slowly as if I were a queen."

---Marilyn Monroe

CHAPTER 1:
THE GOOD TIME GIRL

It's safe to imagine Gladys was scared. It was 1926 and she was supposed to be starting over. She was an It Girl, a Good Time Girl. The type who would show a fella a good time and the type he wouldn't say hello to on the street the rest of the time.

No matter. It was freedom. Women could vote and many of them—Gladys included—wanted all the rights men had and that included the right to enjoy recreational sex.

The problem was, if she'd been a man she could have had all the fun she wanted and she'd never have to pay the price.

She was pregnant and had no idea who the father was. As she confided to her best friend, Grace: it could have been just about anyone.

Grace had been a supervisor at Consolidated Film Industries when she met Gladys, a tall, mousy haired two time divorcee. They'd clicked right away and it was Grace who got her to dye her hair cherry red, who took her to jazz joints, who showed her how much fun was out there.

Eight hours of sitting, white-gloved, in an unventilated room, head pounding from the chemical smell, eight hours of snipping and passing along film negatives without number. After that a gal needed some fun. She loved to dance, loved to drink, and enjoyed doing both of those things, and quite a bit more, with men she knew and with men she barely knew.

Maybe she could have taken precautions but that was easier said than done. Birth control was still illegal in the United States, even for married women. But they at least could get their doctors to write a prescription for 'organ sheaths' or 'womb protectors'. FOR HYGIENE PURPOSES the prescription would read and those women could pretend it was true and the pharmacist, reading the words, would pretend right along with them. For a single woman, it was a different game. She'd have to pick those things up off the shelf and face a cashier who'd look at her like she was a two-bit whore.

Of course a girl couldn't very well claim to have been swept away if she'd done all that preparation beforehand. Not that you or the fella would be likely to remember to use the damn things once you'd had a few belts of booze.

Gladys hadn't planned on being a mother again. She'd

dropped out of school at age 15 and taken a husband ten years older. Within three months she was bored and decided she couldn't give up other men. Jasper was her second husband and they'd had two kids, a boy and a girl. Neighbor friends took care of them, sometimes for up to twelve hours a day, and when she told Jasper she wanted a divorce, he called her unfit, packed up their two children, and took them back home to Kentucky. A year later, when she'd finally been able to go see them, neither child recognized her. She took the train back to Hollywood alone.

Not knowing what to do now that she was expecting again, and this time on her own, she asked her mother, Della, for help, but Della was busy. She was getting ready to leave for a grand tour of Southeast Asia with her current boyfriend, a Shell Oil executive. She was out of the country when Gladys went into labor. Her coworkers pooled their money to pay for the hospital bill and on June 1, 1926, the baby stopped being just an idea and became a squirming little girl, a tiny thing with a heart shaped face and blue eyes looking up at her.

Gladys named the baby Norma Jeane.

On the hospital forms Gladys lied and said the two children she'd had before were deceased. She lied again when she listed her first husband, Ed Mortensen, as the baby's father. The last time they'd seen each other had been 10 months before, but she had to write something; she couldn't very well leave the space blank.

Two of the married ladies from the factory said they'd love to adopt the baby girl but Gladys told them No. She was done losing children.

Her mother, Della, returned home and had an idea. She knew a couple named Bolender who lived a few blocks away. Nice people, churchy types. Stay at home wife, postman husband. They took in foster children. Gladys could keep her job and the baby would have a stable home until Gladys could get her life together.

And so Norma Jeane went to live with the Bolenders when she was 12 days old.

CHAPTER 2:
BEGINNINGS

For the next seven years Norma Jeane lived with Ida and Wayne Bolender. The stock market crash of 1929 happened when she was five months old but had little effect on her early life. Mr. Bolender, as a postman, was able to maintain steady work and their home, already nice by anyone's standards, was fully paid for. Norma Jeane had her own room, her own toys, and was kept spotlessly clean. She had safety and consistency but received more care than affection.

Her first words, first steps, all of them were for the Bolenders. When she tried to call them Mama and Papa she was gently corrected. Mrs. Bolender told her they helped take care of her but that Gladys was her mother. The small Norma Jeane was confused, as she thought of Gladys only as 'the lady with the red hair' who visited occasionally.

Della was no longer advising Gladys about what to do. She'd been suffering from acute myocarditis and was seen by doctors only once or twice and they prescribed medications which she often forgot to take. It's believed she suffered a stroke in the early months of 1930. Her condition was made worse by frequent respiratory infections which caused a lack of oxygen to her brain, making her hallucinate. She was suffering from congestive heart disease and her condition would cause her to have some periods of intense pain and lack of energy and other times of near ecstasy, mainly due to the fact she was having temporary relief from the pain.

Around the time of Norma Jeane's first birthday Della woke in the middle of the night and had a sudden urge to see her granddaughter. She walked to the Bolenders and when she found the door locked, she broke a window and climbed inside. The Bolenders woke to find Della shoving a pillow down on the baby's face, seeming to try to smother her. The police were called and Della was transported to the state asylum where she died less than a month later.

All Gladys understood was that her mother had died a raving lunatic and she assumed some sort of mental illness must be to blame. She added this misinformation about her mother to the misinformation she already had about her father. He'd died when Gladys was only eight years old and Della had explained he had gone crazy.

When her parents had still been married her father was a railroad worker and had temporarily relocated the family to Mexico so he could work on the Mexican National Railway. A year later they moved back to L.A. and he began having violent mood swings and seizures and then became semiparalyzed. He had developed neurosyphilis, a condition caused not by any sort of sexual activity but by a parasite that had been common in the unsanitary conditions where he'd been living and working. Within months of the onset of his symptoms he was hospitalized and thirty days later he was dead. The only thing Della understood about his condition was that he'd died insane and so that was the only part she told her children.

While Gladys already felt doomed to inherit mental illness from her father's side, she now believed it ran on her mother's side as well. To her it seemed only a matter of time before she lost her mind. It's possible this was her reason for keeping her distance from her baby daughter.

Then something happened to change her way of thinking. Her younger brother Marion, who had married and had three children, did what was known at that time as a 'quick fade.' He told his wife he was going out for a newspaper and then never came back. It made Gladys ashamed to think how he'd abandoned his family. She took a second job, at another film lab, and began to save her money.

She also began to see Norma Jeane more often. By the time the child was a toddler Gladys was seeing her nearly every weekend. The two of them would take one of the city's many trolleys and would visit the beach or one of the many marketplaces where there were tasty things to eat and street performers to see. Sometimes they'd go to the movies and Norma Jeane was one of many children captivated by a brand new cartoon character named Mickey Mouse.

As an adult Marilyn would often say that during her childhood no one ever told her she was pretty but this is untrue. From a young age her mother often told her how pretty she was and how pretty she was going to be someday. Her friend Grace agreed, and so did all the people at the film lab where she'd sometimes visit.

It's probably more accurate to say the Bolenders didn't prize physical beauty to the level that her mother and Grace did. The Bolenders were Pentacostal Christians and stressed to Norma Jeane that the way a person lived while on Earth would determine whether they went to Heaven or Hell. She was taught to pray every night before bed and attended church twice during the week and again on Sundays.

At home and in church Norma Jeane was taught it was sinful to drink, smoke, chew gum, swear, dance, or go to the movies. On Saturdays she loved it when Gladys would take her to those very same movies and they sat in the dark, watching a magic world.

The Bolenders took care not to overstep their boundaries; they never said anything to Gladys about the movies and in return, Gladys never said anything to them about the things they taught Norma Jeane about religion. It's likely there was some confusion in the little girl's head but she seemed satisfied to understand there were lots of ideas about what Good was.

Besides, Gladys and Grace reminded her that the movies made a lot of people feel better. As the Depression wore on, movies became more important than ever before. People needed happy images to keep in their heads. Ticket prices were kept low and people all across America flocked to theatres. They saw kings and pirates and cowboys. Many theatres held weekly lotteries with a chance to win a jackpot. Others offered a weekly 'Dish Night' and quite a few families, collecting one piece per week, were able to accumulate a full set of fine china this way. With movies, people forgot their troubles, or at least tried to.

The Bolenders were strong believers in independence and so when Norma Jeane was old enough to begin school, they simply gave her directions: go two blocks up and go to the first building on the left. She enjoyed school. The Bolenders had taught her how to sit quietly and her mother had taught her how to have fun; school seemed to be a little bit of both of these things at the same time. She had a black and white dog named Tippy and he'd follow her to school each morning and would wait for her outside until he could follow her back home again.

At school the other children played many games involving imagination. When Norma Jeane asked her mother about this, both she and Grace seemed to think dreaming was an important thing to do.

Near the end of the second grade, a neighbor, angry with Tippy's barking, shot the dog and Norma Jeane became hysterical. The Bolenders called her mother and Gladys came and held the child and helped her bury her pet. Gladys had some exciting news. Norma Jeane was going to come live with her in their very own house.

Mrs. Bolender asked Gladys when and Gladys told her "Right now, today."

She didn't want to waste any more time. She wanted her little girl home with her.

CHAPTER 3:
GLADYS FALLS

As a single parent, Gladys had qualified for a mortgage with the new Home Owner Loan Corporation. She purchased a white bungalow with one bedroom for her and Norma Jeane and an extra one which she rented out to a British couple named Atkinson who were active in vaudeville. At age seven Norma Jeane was beginning what was probably the happiest year of her life and the only time the word 'home' would mean anything to her.

Grace visited often and the group had a wonderful time; everyone fawned over Norma Jeane. The British couple found her delightful and taught her how to hula hoop and juggle oranges. Often the adults rolled back the rugs, put on music, and danced and laughed and didn't care how late it got.

It was summertime and while Gladys was at work Norma Jeane would sit all day long in darkened movie theatres. Later she would recall how she loved these afternoons and never got tired of watching the movies, even the ones she saw over and over again. Many of the theatres themselves were as entertaining as the movie playing inside. The Egyptian had real looking sphinxes and mummy cases and Grauman's Chinese Theatre had the sidewalk full of the hand and footprints of movie stars. Gladys and Norma Jeane took turns trying to figure out whose feet their feet matched. Sometimes the films were the silent ones and sometimes they were Talkies.

They watched Rudolph Valentino and Lillian Gish and her mother's favorite, Jean Harlow. Both Grace and Gladys seemed to think Norma Jeane was like the platinum blonde actress and could follow in her footsteps. Before the child could really understand what the phrase meant the two women taught her to announce "I'm going to be a movie star," and they dressed her up and took her to the film lab often so she could repeat this line to their coworkers who would always smile and nod, no matter how many times the women brought the little girl in. When going to the movies Gladys and Grace put a tiny bit of rouge and lipstick on Norma Jeane because, as they told her, going out was a special occasion.

After about a year of this happy routine, Gladys received news which was to alter their lives considerably. Her grandfather had committed suicide. Otis Baker, who had been divorced by Della's mother and who hadn't seen his children in years, had begun to have serious health problems: his kidneys and liver had begun to fail and daily activities became very difficult. He learned about his middle child, Della's, death the same month he learned the bank was repossessing his farm. Unable to cope, he hung himself from a beam in the barn.

Although Gladys had never met her grandfather, news of his death, and also the manner of his death, struck her hard. Instead of focusing on the multiple stressors he'd been facing, she only focused on the concept of suicide as being proof of mental illness.

In fact, at that time, there were many suicides. It was one year away from the very worst year of the Depression and 1 out of every 5 American men were out of work. The newspapers became used to a certain number of suicides being reported each week. It was a sad reality of the time.

And Gladys, who already believed both her father and mother had carried mental illness in their genes, now added her grandfather to the mix. Her manner changed abruptly. She lost all energy to get out of bed and wept throughout the day, worrying Grace and frightening Norma Jeane. Little was known about the benefits of counseling at that time and it was a service unavailable in Los Angeles. After three weeks, lacking any other ideas, Grace brought a neurologist to the house. He gave Gladys a tranquilizer which caused an allergic reaction. Immediately after the dose, Gladys suffered violent seizures and began to have symptoms she'd never had before: almost total withdrawal from what was going on around her and crying and laughing at odd moments and for no reason.

Much of the time she spent simply lying in her bed, awake but not responding to Norma Jeane, who begged her to come back. Gladys, no longer able to clean or dress herself, lost her job and needed full time care. She was placed in a nursing home at age 32.

For the next year the vaudeville couple lived in the house alone with Norma Jeane and they cared for her the best they could. School started again and Grace came over every weekend to visit and take the little girl to the movies, to get her mind off things.

The Atkinsons were unable to find work in L.A. and told Grace they were moving back to England. Already in financial trouble without Gladys' income, Grace couldn't make the mortgage payments.

Just when she already had her hands full, the nursing home notified Grace they couldn't keep Gladys any longer. Although she frequently seemed withdrawn and quiet, her symptoms were no longer severe enough to meet their criteria.

Grace, who had already been prepping Norma Jeane for future movie stardom, began the steps to become her legal guardian. For some reason her plans never seemed to include Norma Jeane living with her, only with her consulting and advising the child and arranging for her care.

Grace learned that, in order to get guardianship, a judge would have to declare Gladys insane and then Norma Jeane would have to spend at least six months in an orphanage. And so Grace testified that Gladys had seemed quite depressed after learning of her grandfather's suicide and that she had also been upset when her mother had died only one year earlier. Yes, she slept a lot. Yes, she had lost a little weight. The judge also took the fact that Gladys had had a child out of wedlock as evidence of mental illness.

It was at this time Gladys received a surprising phone call at the nursing home. Her first husband, Ed Mortensen, whom she believed had died in a motorcycle accident years earlier, called her one day, out of the blue. The Ed Mortensen who had died had been a stranger with the same name. Edward expressed a wish to help her out financially and help her get into her own home. They arranged a time to meet but when the nursing home saw Gladys leaving they viewed it as 'escaping'. When she explained Ed had called and she had to go meet him, they reminded her that her file had him listed as deceased. DELUSIONAL, they wrote in her file. Gladys tried to tell them she'd spoken to him by phone. HALLUCINATING, they wrote down. This event, and the chart notes it inspired, sealed Gladys' fate and she was declared legally incompetent. She was sent to live at the Norwalk State Hospital, the place where each of her parents had died.

CHAPTER 4:
PACKING A SUITCASE

Grace was unhappy at the thought of Norma Jeane having to live at an orphanage and convinced the court she could find foster care for her for the six month period. The court agreed and Grace reported this to a relieved Norma Jeane. Grace stressed what good news this was, that she wouldn't have to go live with strangers. She promised the child she'd never have to worry about the orphanage again and Norma Jeane believed her.

She placed the child in the home of a friend's mother. It was to be the first of several foster homes, although at each of them Norma Jeane had previously met the adults, who were always either friends or relatives of Gladys or Grace. She was never told how long she'd be at each house, only finding out it was time to leave when she was told to go pack her suitcase. In the third grade alone she moved five separate times. Still, she kept doing well in school, only seeming dumb when someone asked her address and she had to stop and think.

At the age of nine she was living with a friend of Grace's who ran a boarding home. One day, while restocking towels in a linen closet, one of the older male renters asked her to come into his room. An obedient child, Norma Jeane did as she was told. He offered her candy and then sexually assaulted her. Afterward, as the little girl was sobbing, he put a nickel into her hand and told her, "Go get yourself an ice cream." Norma Jeane threw the nickel at the man and ran from the room.

She found her foster mother and told her what had just happened and the woman slapped her, hard, across the face. "How dare you say those things about that nice man!" she yelled at the child and Norma Jeane opened her mouth to try to explain but all that came out was a stutter. She ran to her room and cried herself to sleep and was comforted by no one. From that moment on, the stutter would reappear whenever she was upset or nervous, and it would continue for the rest of her life.

The next foster home was with her Aunt Olive, the one who had been abandoned at the height of the Depression and left to care for a farm and three children. Olive had looked into it and found there were state assistance programs to help women in her position. The first step was to hire a private investigator to try to find the missing husband. When he couldn't, you had to have the husband declared legally dead. (Not that he was, mind you. He was off somewhere living fancy free while the woman was explaining to her children how they'd have to repeat this version.) The second step was more difficult: the 10 year mandatory waiting period before any food or financial benefits would begin. Norma Jeane was aware she was an extra mouth to feed and felt some relief when Grace told her she could leave.

Grace had met a man named Doc and after a month of successful romancing, had gone with him to Las Vegas for a quickie wedding. He had three daughters of his own and Grace and Doc returned with one of his daughters to live in Los Angeles.

The original plan was that Norma Jean would live with them, but five weeks into this arrangement Doc decided he couldn't afford the expense of four people, and so Grace told Norma Jeane to go pack her suitcase and the two of them got into the car. Grace drove for a long time and Norma Jeane tried to ask where they were going but Grace just stared straight ahead and made no reply.

Norma Jeane didn't see the sign until after they'd pulled over and she was out of the car.

LOS ANGELES ORPHANS HOME SOCIETY

It was the orphanage.

Norma Jeane cried and begged Grace, "Please, please don't make me go inside. I'm not an orphan!" but Grace continued to say nothing. Hysterical, the weeping Norma Jeane collapsed on the sidewalk. Grace physically dragged the child into the building and then left.

30

CHAPTER 5:
BECOMING THE "MMM" GIRL

Sixty children between the ages of 16 months and 18 years were residents at the Los Angeles Orphans Home Society, a stately looking group of brick buildings which, at first glance, could easily be mistaken for a private school. There was one dorm for boys and one for girls, six children to each room. In 1935 fully one third of the children living there were in the same shoes as Norma Jeane: they had at least one living parent who couldn't financially support them. Another large group was made up of children of migrant workers who, facing starvation themselves, had placed their children where they'd be sure to have three meals a day, and a roof, and a bed.

The staff cared tremendously about the children but also kept appropriate boundaries. There were parties and Christmas presents, picnics at the waterfront property owned by the orphanage, and day trips to areas of interest. There were no hugs.

Each child was given a set of chores proportionate to his or her age. Norma Jeane's chores were to dry dishes for about 30 minutes twice a week and to make her bed every day. The staff believed it made the kids feel useful to help out, and that this was good for their self-esteem. In later years Marilyn would greatly exaggerate her duties while a resident. She would say she had been made to wash "100 dishes, and 100 spoons and 100 forks" but this is untrue. The facility had a fully paid staff to do all of the actual cooking and cleaning.

Each week children who chose to do extra chores were rewarded with a movie, shown at the facility. This particularly bothered Norma Jeane, that anything was required in order for her to see a movie. As she told people years later, when it still bothered her, it would have been different if the prize had been something else: anything except a movie.

The children attended public school and in fact Norma Jeane's school was just down the street. Each day she wore one of two identical outfits—white blouse and blue cotton dress—which was the uniform for girls at the orphanage. Some of the girls didn't mind the uniform because they'd never had such nice clothes before, but to Norma Jeane, it was bad enough she had to live there without it being obvious to anyone who saw her. In time she made friends with other girls her age and she was one of the few residents who had a visitor nearly every weekend.

Grace tried to cheer Norma Jeane up by encouraging her to

think about the future. She'd take her to the beauty parlor and Norma Jeane was one of the few 9 year olds getting weekly $15 hair treatments ($50, by today's standard) at the height of the Depression.

Grace, who had originally come to Hollywood as a rather homely looking peroxide blonde, had once hoped for stardom herself but had quickly accepted it was not to be. Instead, she'd thrown herself into her work at the film lab. Her specialty was observing the process by which the movie studios took ordinary looking men and women and altered their appearance with hair, makeup, plastic surgery, and careful lighting, to transform them into screen gods and goddesses. She herself often did the makeup for the starlets and so she decided to turn her talents to Norma Jeane.

In Grace's opinion, the girl was clearly going to be very attractive, but she'd need to fix the bump on her nose, do something about her chin, and get her teeth fixed. In fact, when Norma Jeane was signed to her first studio contract, years later, those were the first three tasks done, so Grace could be looked at as critical or just plain accurate.

One day she brought a dress for Norma Jeane, took her to the salon, paid for her makeup to be professionally done and had her photos taken at a photography studio. She placed the photos in an album for Norma Jeane to keep, so she herself could see how much potential she already had.

She continued the moviegoing tradition Gladys had started but went one better. Because they were in Hollywood, she and Norma Jeane were sometimes able to stand outside actual premieres, watching their favorite stars walking on the red carpet as flashbulbs popped all around them. One especially thrilling moment for Norma Jeane was seeing Clark Gable strolling by, looking dashing in his tuxedo.

In this way, Norma Jeane saw how screen stars were actually just very good looking people in wonderful clothes.

She began to imagine being one of them.

Norma Jeane stayed at the orphanage 21 months and just before her 11th birthday moved in with Grace and Doc. At school she was described as an average student, getting Bs and Cs in most of her subjects but managing As in secretarial type courses like typing and bookkeeping, a likely enough report card for a girl not on the college tack.

In junior high she joined the glee club and wrote pieces for the school newspaper. Her fellow students found her nice but shy.

That was about to change.

She began noticing boys when she was 13, the same year she started getting a curvy figure. One day, quite by accident, she had to wear a sweater that was two sizes too small and she noticed the boys staring and the girls regarding her as competition. From that day forward, Norma Jeane wore that size sweater all the time. She gave up the offer of a ride to and from school in favor of walking each way, several boys always walking beside her as she listened, with pleasure, to the many drivers honking their horns at her in approval.

She was elected class secretary and was embarrassed that each time she had to read the minutes, the stutter would reappear, causing her to pronounce the word "m-m-minutes." For a brief time she was at risk for being branded with the nickname 'm-m-m-girl', likely the suggestion of a jealous female classmate. Showing an early understanding of PR, Norma Jeane reflected the boys all said "mmm!" when she walked by, so really she WAS the Mmmm girl. The boys happily agreed and this nickname, The Mmmm Girl, appeared beneath her yearbook photo. Years later, as a model, she would still be using the slogan and men would still be agreeing it was a good one.

Around the same time she began noticing boys, her grades went down. When faced with angry teachers Norma Jeane learned mentioning the orphanage worked wonders. In fact she often went one step further and outright lied, saying both of her parents were dead. No one scolded her then. Not only was she given less work to do, she was usually given extra warmth and praise.

Most of her attention was focused on her appearance and getting as much attention as possible. Like most girls in Hollywood at that time, she grabbed as many free samples of cosmetics as her purse would hold and began spending hours getting ready before school each day. She had no desire to blend in; she wanted to stand out. She darkened her brows and wore bright red lipstick. As Norma Jeane saw it, the bigger the reaction, the better she was doing.

When she was 13 she saw a movie called The Wizard of Oz, a story which affected her so strongly she could barely get up out of her chair when the film ended. The idea of Dorothy going from an ordinary world into a magical one was very much something Norma Jeane wanted to do. Of all the movies she had seen before and would see afterward, The Wizard of Oz would remain one of her favorites.

The boys at school weren't the only ones noticing Norma Jeane's changing figure; apparently 'uncle' Doc noticed it too. One night in November the 13 year old Norma Jeane woke up to find a drunk Doc kissing her, shoving his tongue into her mouth and trying to grope her. Grace woke to the sound of the girl's screams and directed her intoxicated husband to leave the room.

There were no repercussions for Doc; it didn't even have a negative effect on his marriage. Grace simply made Norma Jeane pack her suitcase and the next day she was sent to yet another relative and had to learn yet another new address.

Unfortunately, the number of friends and relatives willing to take the girl in was growing smaller. Three foster homes later, Norma Jeane was living with Grace's Aunt Ana Lower. By early 1942 Ana's health was failing and Grace and Doc were preparing to move to West Virginia for his job. Whether or not Norma Jeane would have wished to go with them wasn't considered; they told her they couldn't afford to take her in.

Grace assured Norma Jeane she was working on a surprise that would solve the housing problem.

CHAPTER 6:
GOING TO THE CHAPEL

The surprise was going to be an arranged marriage between Norma Jeane and the son of a neighbor. In late 1941 the 20 year old Jim Dougherty was working at Lockheed Aircraft and although he'd met Norma Jeane a few times, had never thought of her as dating material. His mother had explained it to him: in the spring the girl would be 16 and if they didn't get married, she'd have to go back to live at the orphanage for another two years.

Years later, Jim would state, "I agreed to it because I was going into the service soon and I figured she'd have a home with my mother. And of course I thought she was an adorable girl who was fun to be with. I didn't really think much beyond that. And Norma Jeane went along with the idea."

Norma Jeane would recall it differently: "They couldn't support me and they had to work out something."

During their two month engagement she worried about the wedding night. In the 1940s there was no sex education, only a

tradition of older female relatives giving the young bride-to-be one of many Marriage Instruction Manuals. These booklets explained the horrifying things their husbands might do to them in bed.

After studying the manual, Norma Jeane sat with Jim, his mother, and Grace, drinking Coca-Colas on the back porch. She asked them if maybe she and Jim could get married without the sex part. The group laughed and Grace assured the girl she'd learn.

On June 19th, two and a half weeks after her 16th birthday, she became Mrs. Jim Dougherty. The ceremony was performed by a minister in a friend's living room, with a reception at a nearby restaurant. Neither Grace nor Gladys attended the event, but the Bolenders were there, which was better than nothing.

After they married Norma Jeane learned what her husband liked but found sex gave her no pleasure at all. She tried to imitate what she thought a wife should try to be like but didn't fit in the role. She couldn't cook, misspent his money, and seemed like the child she in fact was. Jim liked that he could show off her picture to his coworkers (including the future actor Robert Mitchum) but disliked it when his wife deliberately wore clothing two sizes too small that got her second and third glances everywhere she went.

Because his job at Lockheed was considered essential to the war effort, Jim could have kept his military deferment and remained stateside but he wanted to be overseas, where his buddies were enjoying all the action. Norma Jeane begged him to at least let her have a baby so she wouldn't be so lonely, but he refused. As he explained, she could barely take care of herself, let alone care for a baby.

Jim arranged for Norma Jeane to move in with his mother who worked as a nurse at the Radioplane Company and she got a job for Norma Jeane, spraying varnish on fuselage fabric. For work she wore the same ugly jumpsuit as everyone else but hers hugged her figure, thanks to some careful alterations. She saw no reason she shouldn't look as good as possible all the time.

Photographers from the Army's First Motion Picture Unit had been told to go get shots of women contributing to the war effort. The pictures would be used in commercial and military magazines. 25 year old photographer David Conover noticed Norma Jeane and began snapping photos.

He introduced himself with a question: "Where the hell have you been?"

CHAPTER 7:
BECOMING

Conover had his own studio and knew a natural talent when he saw one. Norma Jeane's skin was luminescent; it came through in every photo, and in each photo, she looked slightly different. He recommended she go into modeling and by the time she left work that day, she felt like a different person.

She began modeling for Conover and was in a hurry to make up for lost time. Each day she'd study photos of herself and would ask him why she looked good in this one, why she looked awkward in that one. She learned her angles. She posed in barnyards and in the mountains and on the side of the highway. She learned not to shiver in the snow and not to squint in direct sunlight. Whatever was asked of her, she did.

She studied fashion magazines and practiced posing, and took photos of herself at home, working especially hard on how to make

her somewhat short legs appear longer.

In 1944 she took a solo trip to Chicago to visit Grace, who was somewhat worse for wear. She was temporarily separated from Doc and had developed a noticeable drinking problem. She also took the train to Tennessee to finally meet her half-sister. Norma Jeane hadn't been told Berniece even existed until she was 12. Since then, the two had exchanged letters and photos, eager to make up for lost time. In Berniece Norma Jeane finally had someone who understood just how it was, trying to cope with Gladys.

Berniece too had tried to have some connection to her long lost mother and had learned to accept any relationship with Gladys would be limited in depth and somewhat uncomfortable. In the years that would follow Berniece would be a valuable peer to her sister, understanding completely how Norma Jeane, like herself, wanted and deserved a life of her own, and that neither of them could provide the level of assistance their mother required. The wishing for their real mother to be anything like the one they kept in their memory: no one else could understand that like a sister.

When Jim returned for a Christmas visit in 1944 he listened to Norma Jeane raving about the fun she was having modeling and decided not to take it too seriously. At least it kept her busy and she wasn't asking to have a baby anymore.

By January of 1945 she had quit her job at Radioplane and spent a happy spring and summer posing for Conover. Her mother in law became concerned this wasn't proper behavior for a married woman and wrote a letter to her son, telling him so. In response, Norma Jeane moved out of her mother in law's home and into her own apartment where she could do as she pleased.

A letter from Jim came next:

'…All of this business of modeling is fine but when I get out of the service we're going to have a family and you're going to settle down. You can only have one career and a woman can't be in two places at once…'

Norma Jeane stopped writing him. And then, deciding her wedding vows were somewhat open to interpretation, she had an affair with Conover.

By August of 1945 she was one of 18 models signed to the prestigious Blue Book Modeling Agency of Los Angeles and was told she needed to lose ten pounds. That was according to Miss Emmaline Snively, who owned the agency. The Britishwoman told her quite frankly that she was too fat and that there wasn't enough upper lip between the end of her nose and her mouth.

There was more: the hair was disaster. She'd have to change it with straightening and then bleaching it from the dull brown into blonde. She explained to Norma Jeane that blonde hair would mean she could photograph well in any light. That convinced her. She was sent off to the salon and emerged a blonde. That night she stared at herself in the mirror, fascinated at the difference it made.

None of these changes bothered Norma Jeane, who was having the time of her life. The ten pounds came off, partly from eating less and partly from getting up early in the morning and

jogging along the sidewalks and on the sandy beach where there was more resistance. She began lifting light weights and from that point onward would have a set of them beneath a bed or couch of every place she lived.

Norma Jeane was sent home from her first assignment, posing for the Montgomery Ward clothing catalogue. After a day of shooting they saw how every photo made the viewer look at her instead of at the clothes. That's how Miss Snively realized Norma Jeane belonged on magazine covers. By the spring of 1946 she had appeared on the covers of 33 magazines including US Camera, Parade, Glamorous Models, Personal Romances, Peek, and See.

One day the agency made a short film of her posing in swimsuits and dresses. In these silent movies Norma Jeane looks directly into the camera, batting her lashes, smiling as if in love. Had Jim seen these films he might have known: she wasn't Norma Jeane anymore.

In his opinion, a lot of things weren't going right. When he'd returned in December Norma Jeane was an hour late meeting him and then chattered on and on about that film the agency had made, saying it had been the most exciting day of her life. Jim listened and said nothing; he'd thought the most exciting day of her life had been their wedding day. Then he couldn't get the needed repairs for his car because she needed money for clothes for a modeling trip with some fancy photographer.

In fact she went on two separate trips with the 32 year old

French photographer Andre de Dienes. They traveled to different locations for their photos: Zuma Beach, the Mojave desert, Yosemite, and even Mt. Hood in Oregon State. They got along beautifully and enjoyed a brief affair.

Near the end of their second trip Grace had arranged for Norma Jeane to have a visit with her mother, who had been living in Portland. Gladys had been discharged from the San Francisco clinic with $200 and two dresses and had spent a year wandering around the Pacific Northwest, sometimes homeless, sometimes staying with the Salvation Army.

They had a lunch during which Gladys remained spookily silent until the end and then she asked Norma Jeane if she could live with her. Not knowing what to say, or what Jim would say about the idea, Norma Jeane agreed to think about it.

In February she met another photographer and had another affair. She believed it helped her self-confidence and that this came through in the photos. Indeed, photos taken at this time show a model who is happy to share her deliciousness with the viewer.

In April she sent money to her mother to come live with her. It was a difficult decision but she didn't know what else to do. They slept side by side in the apartment's one bed and when Jim came home for a visit he complained Norma Jeane had planned it that way, to show him there was no room for him in her life. Why else, he said, would she have picked the one month he was due home for a visit? He stayed long enough for a few angry comments and then left to stay at his mother's.

Gladys seemed to enjoy the time she spent with Norma Jeane but found the activities of daily life to be exhausting. One day she made an exception. She got up early and took great care picking out her clothes and fussing with her hair and lipstick. All by herself she took the bus to the Blue Book Modeling Agency and took a short meeting with Miss Snively, just long enough to thank her for all she'd done for Norma Jeane.

Hearing about this later, Norma Jeane was touched beyond words. That one day trip was all Gladys could muster and by the end of the month, Norma Jeane helped her get into a Northern California clinic and she paid monthly for her mother's care from that point onward.

In mid-May Norma Jeane went to visit Grace's Aunt Minnie in Las Vegas. Grace had recruited Minnie to help work on Norma Jeane's future and Minnie educated the girl on the ins and outs of getting a Las Vegas divorce. Two weeks later Norma Jeane filed for divorce from Jim. He immediately took the steps to stop sending her his monthly check and this confused her. To her way of thinking, she saw no reason for him to stop giving her his pay just because she was divorcing him.

She called him from a Las Vegas hospital where she'd just had surgery for a mouth infection. Her speech was slow and her voice wasn't the squeaky one he remembered: it was much lower.

"I remember thinking it was the medication," he would later say.

She explained it was her new professional voice. By slowly

enunciating each word (what one journalist would later describe as "ar-tic-yew-lay-shun") she'd sound sexy. By lowering the pitch, she'd control the stutter.

Norma Jeane decided to make it a little more useful. She practiced forming her words while pushing her lips outward, like you'd do right before kissing someone. This trick would make it impossible for photographers to take her picture mid-sentence, only when she was still and looking her best.

Divorce law required she spend from May 14 to Sept 13 in Las Vegas but on July 17th she flew to Los Angeles. Minnie had used her contacts to arrange for an introduction to Ben Lyon, talent recruiter and casting director for Twentieth Century Fox. He asked Norma Jeane to return in two days for a silent screen test.

CHAPTER 8:
THE FAVOR GAME

The day of her test she met makeup artist Allen "Whitey" Snyder, a person who would become a friend for the rest of her life. Norma Jeane was nervous but he assured her it was a silent test: all she had to do was look beautiful.

On film, Norma Jeane walked across the room and back again. Sat on a stool. Lit a cigarette. Gazed at the camera and smiled.

The men in the room had risked their jobs to do this favor, letting her do a screen test without prior consent from their boss. Watching her, they relaxed, and knew they wouldn't be getting in trouble.

Cinematographer Leon Shamroy would later describe what it was like to watch Norma Jeane's screen test:

'I got a cold chill. This girl had something I hadn't seen since silent pictures. She had a kind of fantastic beauty like Gloria

Swanson, when a movie star had to look beautiful, and she got sex on a piece of film like Jean Harlow.'

It was also viewed by production chief Darryl F. Zanuck, who was less impressed. Marilyn had no on screen experience and had never studied acting. He also preferred brunettes. The studio already had Betty Grable and so in his opinion, they were covered in the blonde department. Agreeing she might have some talent, he instructed the legal department to draw up a standard six month contract at $75/week, with the studio's option to renew.

Days before signing the final contract on August 24, 1946, Lyon said she needed a new, professional name. Norma Jeane wanted to use Monroe because it had been her mother's maiden name. He liked that; it had been the last name of a president and sounded All-American. Lyon chose the first name Marilyn.

"I guess I'm Marilyn Monroe then," she told him. She only had a moment of anxiety later as she confessed to Minnie, "I don't even know how to spell Marilyn!" She spent the rest of the evening practicing signing her new first name.

Being a contract player meant Marilyn would get the same weekly paycheck whether she worked or not and in return, would appear in any film they gave her. Like all of the other contract players, she took free lessons right there on the studio lot so she'd be able to appear in a wide variety of movies. There were dance lessons, voice lessons, mime lessons, and even horseback riding lessons.

Most of the contract players hoped to get a part as an extra.

Getting even one line was difficult, and without getting any chance to even speak on camera, it would make it very hard to prove, within the initial six month contract period, that they had enough talent to stay on the studio's roster.

It seemed it would be important to gain the favors of people in positions of power. That lesson, a disappointment to so many, was one Marilyn accepted without hesitation.

A new actor's fate would also be decided by a group known as 'flacks', the 90 person press and publicity staff at the studio. It was their job to place articles about these newcomers in newspapers and movie magazines, to generate public interest. The publications most prized at that time were Photoplay, Modern Screen, and Silver Screen, and the highly influential newspaper columnists to charm were Hedda Hopper, Louella Parsons, Walter Winchell, and Sidney Skolsky.

Getting and keeping attention wasn't going to be a problem for Marilyn. She'd been training for that part of the job for years. Naturally, every new actress would be trying to get attention too so it would be important to be inventive and maybe just a little bit shocking.

Those other girls never stood a chance.

Inventive she was. Marilyn decided she was dissatisfied with her 35-24-36 measurements and quickly learned tricks to make her bust appear larger. Wearing sweaters two sizes too small, she'd already been doing that, and now she added falsies inside her bra. She was quite fearful of getting sagging breasts if she went braless (she even wore a bra to bed each night) but desired the braless look. To her delight she found this could be accomplished one of two ways: she could sew falsies (which included false nipples) onto the outside of the bra or she could sew strategically placed buttons onto the outside of the bra. To the dressmakers at the studio she was a 35D but to the press she stated 37D.

That covered the top half. For the bottom half, she learned another trick. By slicing one half inch off the heel of one shoe, it made her hips sway a little more when she walked and provided extra bounce. Not that her backside wasn't memorable enough, due to her form fitting skirts. She continued to look luminescent all the time, thanks to the thin layer of Vaseline she always applied to her face before applying foundation.

In August of 1946 Marilyn was one of several starlets sent across the street to the Chevont Hills Country Club's celebrity golf tournament. These starlets were used as pretty caddies for Hollywood biggies including Jimmy Stewart, Henry Fonda, John Wayne, and Tyrone Power.

Marilyn would see Tyrone Power again, under humiliating circumstances. According to Heddy Lamar, Power would host grand parties, staging what he called a "greyhound race" for his guests. Four men with numbers taped to their backs would be the 'greyhounds' and would run on hands and knees after a topless starlet who was the 'rabbit.' The man who caught the girl got a kiss and a photo taken with her and the girl was rewarded with a fur coat. On at least one occasion Marilyn was the 'rabbit' and ran while they chased her and while the biggest stars in Hollywood stood, dressed to the nines, drinks in hand, watching her topless and running on all fours because that was what a girl had to do if she wanted to become a movie star.

In the Hollywood of that time, the so-called casting couch was avoidable for only a lucky few. For everyone else, the deal was made quite clear and this requirement wasn't just for young actresses, but for young actors as well. Many of those who gave in and played the game were the very same names that would later blaze across screen in starring roles.

This group often found themselves in a no-win situation: continue to be exploited for the chance at fame or go back to their hometowns carrying the greasy feel of their experiences with nothing to show for them. Of the few who became stars, many would succumb to self-destructive behavior in the form of reckless driving, drugs, or alcohol abuse.

Walking the nighttime streets of Hollywood, Marilyn let men pick her up for quickies in their cars or alleyways. She refused to ever let them give her money and instead had the man go into a restaurant and pre-purchase her a large meal. Because the men never handed her money directly, she regarded herself not as a call girl but as a girl who needed regular meals. With her own money she paid for her rent, car, and acting lessons.

Nor was she the only starlet making her extra money this way. Hollywood was packed with gorgeous hopefuls and sleeping with men for money or favors was the accepted rule. At least they knew they weren't the only ones; more girls Did than Didn't. The agents of these starlets did nothing to change this circumstance; they merely got the girl's tubes tied. Not only would this prevent an unwanted (and career ending) pregnancy, it was much cheaper, in the long run, than the repeated abortions. Still quite illegal, they cost a pretty penny, especially if you wanted to get it done by an actual doctor.

During her six month studio contract Marilyn appeared in two films: Scudda Hoo! Scudda Hay! (in which she had one scene and one line and was easily upstaged by the 8 year old Natalie Wood) and The Dangerous Years (in which she had three scenes and one line).

Officially speaking, the studio was unimpressed with either performance and opted not to renew her contact in August of 1947. Unofficially, Darryl Zanuck's daughter was crying her eyes out because Marilyn had stolen her fiancé, a young man Zanuck had been personally grooming to go into the business. Upon learning of the affair, Zanuck fired them both.

It would be six months before she'd have a new contract, this time through Harry Cohn at Columbia Pictures and as a direct favor to the Fox executive Marilyn had slept with. Cohn gave her a six month contact at $125/week beginning March 9, 1948, and also got her an acting coach, Natasha Lytess.

In July Marilyn had a fairly substantial role in a somewhat poorly received musical called Ladies of the Chorus. In the film she used her newly acquired skill of dancing and belted out a sweet but vampy song called Every Baby Needs A Da-Da-Daddy. She'd been coached by the studio's musical arranger, Fred Karger. He was freshly divorced and the father of a young son. Fred and Marilyn had a romance for over a year but he broke it off, explaining he could never marry her because if something ever happened to him, she wouldn't be a fit influence for his child. Some women might have been offended by this remark but Marilyn just seemed sad. She wondered if what he said might be true.

A few months later, she got a lucky break in the form of a fender bender. Never the most attentive of drivers, Marilyn rear ended a forgiving fellow named Tom Kelley. He'd been an AP cameraman and had begun an independent photography career with his own studio. He gave her his card.

Marilyn didn't know it yet but Kelley was about to change her life.

CHAPTER 9:
GETTING CLOSER

On New Year's Eve Marilyn met the man who would become her agent: Johnny Hyde, executive VP of the William Morris Agency and one of the most powerful men in Hollywood. Married and the father of two small children, Hyde, 53, fell madly in love with the 22 year old Marilyn. By summer he'd left his family and was begging her to marry him. As he explained, his heart was weak and he had, at best, a year to live. If Marilyn agreed to marry him, he could leave her a fortune and she'd never have to work again.

Many women might have jumped at this offer but Marilyn refused. It was one thing to have a physical affair with Hyde (and she did, thinking it was the least she could do to thank him for all he was doing), but to marry him without being in love with him went against her values.

He purchased a grand home for them to live in and even recreated one area of the house to be an identical match to her favorite restaurant, Romanoff's. Every detail was identical, right down to the tablecloths and bread baskets. Marilyn referred to this as "My own little Romanoff's!" and it made Hyde happy to see her so pleased. He also purchased a separate apartment for Marilyn to use for mail delivery and for appearance's sake.

Hyde completed Marilyn's physical transformation by arranging for a top Beverly Hills doctor to remove the small bump on her nose (noticed by Grace so many years before) and to give her a chin implant. A dentist straightened her teeth and corrected an overbite and the studio used electrolysis to permanently raise the sides of her hairline. This, combined with the chin implant, made her face even more heart shaped.

Hyde also arranged for her to get a tubal ligation, the birth control of preference for stars of the day. He believed it was true, that when removed, she'd be able to have as many children as she wanted. Marilyn believed it too. By this time she'd had at least twelve abortions and didn't realize this had made it virtually impossible for her to ever carry a baby to term.

Her next film would be Love Happy, with the Marx Brothers. Marilyn's audition for the film, as explained to her by Groucho Marx, would be to walk across the room in a way that would make smoke come out of his ears. According to both of them, she successfully did so.

So taken was he with Marilyn, Groucho Marx allowed her to

get fairly high billing for the film even though her appearance consisted of a brief scene with only one line. A trip to New York followed, to promote the film, and Marilyn enjoyed dining at El Morocco and being treated, for the first time, like a star.

Upon returning home, Marilyn called Tom Kelley, the photographer she'd hit with her car, and posed for a Pabst beer magazine ad. A Chicago calendar manufacturer saw the ad and requested she appear in the nude on his upcoming calendar. On Mary 27, 1949, she posed for Kelley. It wasn't the first time she'd posed semi-nude but it was the first time she did so knowing the photos would be published.

Later Marilyn would construct many stories to explain her decision but the truth was, she had many modeling jobs available and no urgent need for money. She posed in the nude because she felt okay posing nude. She signed the contract 'Mona Monroe' and was paid a one-time fee of $50. Kelley was paid a total of $500 for all future publication rights.

Soon afterward, Johnny Hyde had a series of heart attacks. Before he died he was able to secure Marilyn an important part in the John Huston film The Asphalt Jungle and had gotten her a new contract with Fox at $500/week for the first movie and an eventual deal of seven years with a ceiling salary of $1500/week.

Near the end, while confined to his hospital bed, Hyde repeatedly requested Marilyn's presence but she stayed away. Hyde's family told Marilyn she wasn't welcome at his funeral but she came anyway, throwing herself, weeping, on top of his casket.

Later, while filming The Asphalt Jungle, she was found weeping backstage by Elia Kazan and his friend, the playwright Arthur Miller. Miller would later say this initial impression, of the fragile weeping Marilyn, was the one that made him begin to love her.

In the fall she began taking extra drama classes with acting coach Michael Chekhov, nephew of Russian playwright Anton Chekhov and former colleague of Konstantin Stanislavsky at the Moscow Art Theatre. Marilyn began to learn about a new way of acting they were calling, simply, The Method.

Michael confused her somewhat, with his talk about developing an "imaginary body" so her "will" could become another character. Still, it was wonderful to be part of an acting community. She met many New York actors who were in town trying out new plays for west coast audiences. The one thing she did understand about The Method was that it regarded acting as a craft.

During this time Marilyn usually shared an apartment with one girl or another. One roommate would become a lifelong friend. Shelley Winters was in a slightly different boat than Marilyn was. Although she was still slender at that time and had a bit of glamour about her, Shelley had less beauty but far more acting experience and skill and would, in time, go on to win two Academy

Awards*

The two girls had much in common including a size 6 dress size, and they shared a bathing suit for photos and a mink coat for dates. They both loved music and played classical records in the morning and Nat King Cole or Frank Sinatra in the afternoons. They were both quite busy in the man department and spent many a happy evening comparing their conquests, which was made easier by the fact they had slept with many of the same men: the older ones for favors and the younger ones for kicks.

They also shared glamour tricks. Marilyn showed Shelley how to shorten one heel so she could have a sexier walk and Shelley showed Marilyn the trick she'd been using to hide her buck teeth: she'd tilt her head back, lower her eyes, and smile just a little bit, with parted lips.

"I gave her that one," Shelley would later say, smiling.

One night they each made a list of the men they'd like to bed. Marilyn's list was as follows: Zero Mostel, Charles Boyer, Eli Wallach, Jean Renoir, Lee Strasberg, Nick Ray, John Huston, Elia

* when asked to audition, she would pull the two awards from her handbag and set them down on the director's desk and then would ask him, "How did that audition go?"

Kazan, Harry Belafonte, Yves Montand, Charles Bickford, Ernest Hemingway, Clifford Odets, Charles Laughton, Dean Jagger, Arthur Miller, and Albert Einstein.

Marilyn wondered, "Wouldn't it be nice to be like men, just getting notches in your belt, having affairs with the most attractive men…and not getting emotionally involved?"

It seemed like such a smart idea. And then she met Joe.

CHAPTER 10:
JOLTIN' JOE

In 1951 Joe DiMaggio saw a photo of Marilyn standing next to Chicago White Sox players Joe Dobson and Gus Zernial and he liked what he saw. A date was arranged for them at Joe's favorite restaurant, Toot Shorr's. As always, Joe sat at Table One, where only the most important customers were ever seated. It was where Babe Ruth and Ernest Hemingway sat when they were in town. Anyone who sat at Table One received greetings and well wishes from admirers one after the other, the way a king might, were he to be eating pasta.

She arrived two hours late, which for her was actually somewhat early and an indication she was making an effort. She'd expected a loud, crass guy in a cheap sportsjacket but the man waiting for her wore a gray flannel suit and looked more like a politician than an athlete. He said little and gazed at her openly.

They ordered spaghetti and midway through the meal, Mickey Rooney barged in, just sat right down even though nobody'd invited him, and began gushing all over the place: not to Marilyn, but to Joe. This was a new experience for her, not being the focus of attention. Mickey went on and on about how great Joe was, what an amazing player he was, recounting what sounded like every single game he'd ever played.

Marilyn realized this Joe was some kind of big deal.

Joe let Mickey go on for a while and then cast him a single glance that made the little guy disappear, and fast. Marilyn noticed that too. She was glad they were alone again.

The next day the gossip papers ran with the headline "DIMAGGIO STRIKES OUT" because Joe had asked them to. He and Marilyn had spent the night together but he didn't want that in the press. He'd already decided he was going to marry her.

Marilyn ran out and got a copy of that silly Les Brown record, "Joltin' Joe DiMaggio"and soon found herself singing along, with a smile on her face. When Joe would come over, she'd make sure to hide the record so he wouldn't think she was silly.

The pair began dating and for the press, it was Christmas come early. Everyone had something to say about the very attractive pair. Mae West wondered aloud "Why date one player when you can have the whole team?" and an executive from Fox announced "We haven't lost a star, we've gained a center fielder."

Describing Joe as a big deal was something of an understatement. Born Guiseppe Paolo DiMaggio, he was the 8th of 9 children born to a Sicilian family who'd come to America to do the thing their family had done for generations: they were fishermen.

That was the plan for Joe also, but the smell of dead fish made him queasy, causing his father to refer to him as "lazy" and "good for nothing." Those words hurt and Joe escaped the sound of them by spending long hours playing baseball with neighborhood kids in a local truckyard.

By 1936 he'd been signed to the New York Yankees and the boy who had been called "lazy" started to become a legend. He spent a total of 13 years with the team and was an All Star in each of his 13 seasons. A three time MVP winner, Joe helped his team win 10 American League pennants and 9 World Series championships. In 1941, at the peak of his career, he held a 56 game hitting streak, a feat that inspired the nicknames 'Joltin' Joe' and the song of the same name, and an athletic record that still stands to this day.

By 1949 he had become something of a folk hero. His salary had reached an unheard of $100,000 ($995,000, by today's standard) and he was able to buy his parents a big house and invest in a San Francisco restaurant. He drove brand new Cadillacs, wore expensive suits, and lived in New York hotels.

Like Marilyn, he had started from nothing. Their lack of

education, and self-consciousness about it, was another thing they had in common: Joe had left school early so he could work full time to help support his family. Despite his lack of a diploma, Joe had a keen business sense. He was careful with his baseball earnings, had an admirable investment portfolio, and was earning still more money, endorsing products.

But they were at very different places in their careers. Whereas Joe had just retired from baseball, Marilyn's star was still on the rise. And even though they were both famous, the way the press and public treated a star athlete was quite different from the way they treated a movie star. For one thing, when photographers took Joe's picture, they just stood there and snapped the photo. Never once did he have photographers climbing up into trees so they could get a better shot of his body.

Marilyn tried to explain these things to him but he kept insisting it looked like she was constantly bending forward just a little bit, always showing them just a little bit more than she needed to. And because she had taken great pains to hone all of those skills, it was hard for her to try to NOT do them. Especially since they were working so well.

For most of 1952 he encouraged her to quit the movie business. He couldn't understand why she'd want to stay in a career that caused her anxiety. But he was 37 and she was only 25. She wasn't ready to stop doing something she loved. And she was finally beginning to get recognition for her work and much bigger parts.

In the spring of 1952 however, Marilyn had a more immediate problem, although 'problem' probably wouldn't have been the word she would have chosen. The 1951 calendar she'd appeared in had done so well that it had been reprinted for 1952 and a lot of people had noticed the girl in the picture looked a lot like Joe's girlfriend. In fact, a lot of reporters thought so too. Dozens of them had seen the calendar firsthand because Marilyn had mailed it to them.

Posing for the calendar violated the morals clause of her contract with Fox and she was called into the main office, where she confessed she was the calendar girl. The studio decided they'd have Marilyn pretend to confide this fact to a female reporter and would give an explanation about being a girl who just needed the money.

That was how Marilyn explained it, in a hushed voice with make believe tears in her eyes, to UP International correspondent Aline Mosby, who promptly broke the story March 13 in the L.A. Herald Examiner. Within days the story went worldwide. The following month Marilyn appeared on the cover of LIFE magazine, which was exactly the response she'd wanted.

In a way, the scandal was marvelous for everyone. Soon those nude photos appeared in a slew of merchandise: playing cards, beverage trays, keychains, pens, and clothing items. Although Marilyn never received any payment for the photo beyond the initial $50, the PR it gave her was priceless. Several censored versions of the photos appeared. In some she wore a skimpy negligee, in others, a slip. In Japan they made the image wearing a yellow dress. Each time the pictures were shown, banned, or altered, it was a new chance for Marilyn to respond and another time her name was in the papers.

One of the people who had purchased a copy of the calendar was none other than FBI director J. Edgar Hoover. He liked it so much he hung it up on his living room wall and kept it there permanently. Later Hoover would come to have a much different interest in Marilyn but in 1952, he just had the same interest every other man seemed to have.

In the late spring Marilyn was in the press again, this time because someone had learned her mother was alive and living in some kind of mental hospital. Until this time the studio had encouraged Marilyn to state she was an orphan in the literal sense; orphans were very big in the movies at that time. Marilyn responded by giving the press another false story: her father had been killed in a car accident and she had only recently learned that her mother was alive.

Her makeup man, Whitey Snyder, was by now an old friend. One day Marilyn asked him to promise, if she died before he did, that he'd do her final makeup. He agreed. "While I'm still warm!" she teased. The next week she presented Snyder with a gold moneyclip. The engraving read: Whitey Dear, While I'm still warm. –Marilyn.

In June she began work on the film Niagra, the biggest role she'd had yet. That summer, Marilyn met Joe's family in San

Francisco and she got a firsthand look at the kind of traditional life he wanted for them: one she wasn't quite sure she was ready to have. Studio publicists arranged for her to be the first female Grand Marshal of the Miss America parade in Atlantic City and Marilyn wore a dress with a neckline that plunged to just above her navel. Cameras clicked.

In the fall she began filming Gentlemen Prefer Blondes. Her role was originally intended for Betty Grable but Marilyn was just more popular at the box office and Grable herself handled the news admirably, telling Marilyn "Honey, I've had mine—now go get yours."

In the film she was paired with Jane Russell who, coincidentally, had attended the same high school as Marilyn, but in Jimmy's class, not hers. Jane would remain a good friend to Marilyn, offering her friendship and sound business advice.

Also that fall Joe accompanied Marilyn to several L.A. boutiques to personally supervise all of her new wardrobe purchases. Wearing more conservative clothing was one of the rules Joe said she had to follow if they were going to be together. The other was that she should only accept movie roles that presented her in an upstanding way.

Marilyn enjoyed making Gentlemen Prefer Blondes and, to her friends, said she was the star of the movie. When they tried to correct her and say she was ONE of the stars, she'd insist she was right in the title. It was Gentlemen Prefer BLONDES, and she was the blonde.

One musical number in the film seemed especially important to Marilyn, so much so that she insisted they film it 11 times. She was correct: the scene would become one of her most famous onscreen moments. In it, she wore a strapless pink dress and elbow length gloves. Surrounded by tuxedoed men, she gave the world the song Diamonds Are A Girl's Best Friend.

It was a year for making history. That winter of 1953 a 27 year old copywriter for Esquire magazine was told he couldn't get a $5 raise and quit on the spot, vowing to produce his own magazine right out of his Chicago kitchen. The young man was Hugh Hefner and the premiere issue of the magazine he called Playboy cost fifty cents and featured, on its cover, a photo of Marilyn in the low cut dress at the Miss America parade, smiling as she waved to the crowds. He hadn't yet decided on the bunny motif, nor had he thought of the term 'playmate', so Marilyn was referred to as their first "Sweetheart of the Month". As such, the Tom Kelley photo Hefner had purchased became Playboy's first centerfold. 50,000 copies flew off the shelves and everyone who bought one and gazed at the lazily stretched and nude Marilyn felt they'd gotten a pretty good deal for fifty cents.

CHAPTER 11:
THE SHOT SEEN ROUND THE WORLD

When did the abuse begin? Did it start right at the beginning or did it really begin after January 14, 1954, when they married in a quickie city hall ceremony in San Francisco?

When it began is something only Marilyn and Joe could answer. That it happened was a secret to no one. There were shouting matches, of course, lots of people had those, but there was more. The makeup artists on her movie sets began to see bruises on Marilyn's skin, most often on her back and upper arms. They covered the bruises with makeup and said nothing.

Her on again-off again flame Marlon Brando was very upset to see the black and blue marks and he was one of the few people who directly asked her if Joe had done that to her. Marilyn nodded her head and the two said no more.

At that time in America such things were rarely spoken of aloud. It bothered people to know a woman was being abused by a boyfriend or husband but the common practice was to feel sympathy while staying silent and hoping either the situation would improve or that the woman would leave the relationship. No one liked to see the bruises and no one said a critical word about it to Joe.

His own son would later describe waking up to the sounds of Joe and Marilyn fighting and watching as a tearful Marilyn tried to leave by the front door and as his father grabbed her by the hair and dragged her back inside.*

Some people blamed the abuse on the fact that Joe was Italian and therefore, more passionate by nature. Regarding physical abuse as a variety of passion made it sound like some sort of compliment and it certainly placed any blame on the victim. Some people (especially baseball fans) said it made sense: Joe was a first generation Sicilian American who grew up on rough streets in a rough time.

This reasoning was incorrect, as first generation Sicilian American Frank Sinatra could have told them. He'd grown up in the same time, under similar circumstances, and the idea of laying a hand on a woman horrified him. With men he could have a very quick temper and he was known to throw drinks, ashtrays, and alarm clocks against the wall. But hurt a woman? Never.

By this time Marilyn had completed two more films: River Of No Return and How To Marry A Millionaire. In Millionaire she

---

*Fourteen years old by then, Joe Jr. would grow up to beat his own wife so badly that she required hospitalization, after which she divorced him.

was paired with Betty Grable and Lauren Bacall and the press, hoping for backstage bickering, was sadly disappointed: the three bombshells got along easily. The public was by now fascinated with everything Marilyn did and sometimes this led to awkward moments. When reporters learned DiMaggio had specifically requested a television set for the honeymoon suite so that he could follow the baseball games, several members of the press wondered why anyone on a honeymoon with Marilyn Monroe would care if a TV was in the room or not.

Soon after their wedding they traveled to Tokyo where Joe was scheduled to attend exhibition baseball games and rookie training sessions with an old friend. The day they departed for the trip he and Marilyn posed for a few pictures and photographers noticed her thumb was taped and in a splint. When asked about it she told them she'd bumped it and then refused to answer any more questions.

The minute they arrived in Tokyo, it became clear Marilyn was a bigger star than Joe. The thousands of screaming fans at the airport were calling her name, not his. She accompanied him to a press conference and although the event was intended to honor Joe, reporters aimed every question at Marilyn. They didn't seem to care about baseball but did seem interested in finding out what she wore to bed. Never entirely out of publicity mode, Marilyn answered their questions with her typical quick, funny answers and her new husband sat silently, glaring at the room.

The next day General John E. Hall asked if Marilyn might be willing to do a one woman show for servicemen in Korea. When Marilyn asked Joe if it'd be okay, he said "Why not? It's your honeymoon." His voice was filled with a sarcasm that went over her head.

Thinking she had his approval, Marilyn became USO entertainer serial # 129278 and in fact she ended up doing ten separate shows in four days. Traveling by plane, open jeep, and helicopter, bundled up in fatigues and a heavy jacket, Marilyn went from base to base, meeting enlisted men and then delighting them by appearing onstage in a slinky dress. It was freezing outside and she ended up getting a nasty cold afterward, but she understood this was the price for giving a good performance.

She sang Bye Bye Baby and Diamonds Are A Girl's Best Friend for a total of 100,000 soldiers and 13,000 Marines. The majority of these men, due to their deployment, had never seen any of her films and only knew her from movie star magazines and, of course, her calendar.

Asked how she felt to be surrounded by thousands of GIs, Marilyn responded "Safe."

Joe was cool to her for the rest of the trip and when they returned to San Francisco he refused to accompany her to the

Photoplay awards where she won the Best Actress award for the second year in a row. The man she referred to as her "Slugger" was nowhere to be seen.

Meanwhile, Fox had offered her a deal: if she was willing to appear in the musical There's No Business Like Show Business, she could have the lead in the upcoming film The Seven Year Itch.

The idea of appearing alongside musical legends Ethel Merman and Donald O'Connor was intimidating to Marilyn. She'd had singing lessons, of course, and could deliver a tune well enough but she knew she was out of her league. To try her best to prepare for the role she spent hours working with vocal coach Hal Schaefer. This led to rumors in the tabloids of an affair between the two and Schaefer responded to these rumors by calling them 'ridiculous'. To Joe's way of thinking, this was the same as Schaefer calling him ridiculous, giving him another reason to hate the man.

On the night of July 27 Schaefer failed to show for several appointments and his friends, concerned, found him sprawled on the floor of his Fox bungalow at 4am. There had been rumors of anonymous threatening phone calls to Schaefer, telling him to stay away from Marilyn. Schaefer, who appeared to have been viciously beaten, was rushed to the hospital where it was discovered he had ingested a nearly lethal amount of Benzedrine and Nembutal. He himself claimed to have no recollection of events and didn't question the official version that he had attempted suicide and had

somehow beaten himself mercilessly afterward.

He sent word that Marilyn was ready for the movie and would need no further voice lessons.

Marilyn completed the film in a state of misery. Joe appeared only once, took one look at her flashy costumes, and then left without speaking to her. She did her best with the singing and dancing, even while being able to overhear her famous costars laughing at her and ridiculing her from just offstage. She kept her mind on her next film. Something told her The Seven Year Itch was going to be a very important step in her career.

She had tried with Joe. Never having seen a single baseball game prior to their marriage, she learned to watch the sport. She learned to shoot pool. She tried to be interested in the TV Western he liked so much. Somehow she was always disappointing him, falling short of whatever it was he had wanted her to be. She'd toned down her image but she couldn't change everything about herself and wondered why she should have to.

Neither one wanted to do dishes: he because he thought it was women's work and she because she'd usually had a hard work day already and couldn't understand why he wouldn't let them hire a housekeeper. Often her handsome husband refused to speak to her for 5-7 days at a time.

At the end of August Marilyn began work on a film where her character was named, simply, The Girl, and which would place her forevermore in the minds of moviegoers as what sexy looks like.

The Seven Year Itch details the (successful) effort of a decent family man, left on his own for a week while his family is on vacation, to resist the temptation of the beautiful girl who lives upstairs. In this role Marilyn is simultaneously enchanting and innocent, seemingly unaware of the power she has over his fate. She has somehow found a loophole: she is accidentally sexy.

The studio had an idea to increase public interest in the film. They arranged to film a scene outside the Trans-Lux Theatre on Lexington at 52nd Street between 1am-4am on September 15. In this scene the man and Marilyn pause as she stands above a sidewalk subway grate and she is thrilled to feel the whoosh of cool air that blows the skirt of her dress up to waist level.

This event was highly publicized and 5000 spectators set their alarm clocks and braved the cold to see what columnist Irving Hoffman would later describe as "the shot seen round the world."

It would prove to be the event that ended her marriage.

Joe thought it would make Marilyn nervous if he went to the event. That was what he tried to tell his buddy, Walter Winchell, but the columnist (maybe thinking he could get something for his readers) pestered him until he agreed to go.

In the finished film version the scene is shot at waist level and is more comical than sexy. That version would be shot later, on the Fox lot. The supposed filming on 52nd Street was strictly for PR purposes.

And maybe because he thought it was funny (and knew Marilyn well enough by then to know she'd take it with a laugh), he directed the cameramen to shoot from a much lower angle, directly at her panties. The garment was modest enough at first glance but the powerful lights used for the night filming made them completely see through.

The crew (and the many reporters and press photographers present) delighted in this peek-a-boo as Wilder ordered take after take. The men in the crowd were quite enthusiastic about the view, although one photographer standing in front of Joe complained to the man next to him that he'd always thought she was a natural blonde.

Joe pulled Marilyn, roughly, off the set. A furious yelling match ensued and the next day when she arrived to work, she had a fresh set of bruises.

Two weeks later, she filed for divorce.

CHAPTER 12
THE WRONG DOOR RAID

At first Joe refused to take it seriously, but Marilyn stuck to her decision. Per California law the divorce would not be final for another year but the idea that his girl might be unfaithful to him during that year drove DiMaggio wild. He arranged to have her phone bugged and to have her followed by a private investigator. Whereas the average person might not know where to begin to find such services, DiMaggio already knew of several people who could do the job but chose to use an investigator his buddy Frank Sinatra had used and recommended highly.

On November 5, as Joe and Frank sat having dinner at the Villa Capri, this investigator sent word that he'd followed Marilyn to the same apartment building several times. It just happened to be the building where Hal Schaefer lived.

Joe assumed Marilyn was having an affair with Schaefer and he was correct. Frank tried to calm Joe down but finally agreed to go to the address with him. It was a decision he soon came to regret.

Frank, while having many friends and associates who may or may not have had any number of exciting personal activities* had made an art form of keeping his nose clean. In fact, the only time he'd had anything on his record was an arrest when he had been 23 years old and charged with Seduction.

At that time, he'd been found to be having an affair with a married woman. It was only after the woman was revealed to have had prior extramarital affairs that the charge against Frank was dropped. In 1938 corrupting a "good" woman was illegal, but having physical relations with a "fallen" one no longer counted as a crime in the eyes of the law.

So it was with a clean record that Frank, Joe, and five of their most loyal friends, including the Villa Capri maître d', drove to the apartment building and broke down the door of the wrong tenant. Instead of finding Marilyn and Hal, they discovered a screaming 39 year old secretary with curlers in her hair. Seeing their mistake, the group fled.

Marilyn and Hal had heard all the commotion and made a fast exit out the back way. The secretary, a woman named Florence

*including his godfather, Willie Monetti AKA Willie Moore, alleged underboss of the Genovese crime family

Kotz, called the police who, in turn, made sure to keep the stars' names out of the record. The public found out about the incident anyway, when the tabloid Confidential ("Tells The Facts And Names The Names") printed a story about the incident, which they dubbed the Wrong Door Raid. Both Frank and Joe were named in the story, although Joe insisted he'd never been there or known anything about it. Frank eventually paid the woman $7,500 in an out of court settlement even though he denied ever being there either.

By this time Marilyn was close friends with Sidney Skolsky, who kept a casual "office" at Schwab's drugstore, where he could easily observe the comings and goings of Hollywood names for his columns. As an added bonus, the pharmacy staff was happy to give him unlimited free samples of any pills he wanted. These he freely shared with friends, including Marilyn, who by now kept an assortment of them in a plastic baggie she kept in her handbag.

One of her romances had begun at Schwab's: it was where she met Charlie Chaplin Jr. Their affair was short-lived because he came home one day and found her in bed with his brother.

Sidney laughed as she told him the story. Marilyn often gave him free rides around town, and in return he would often surprise her with some new pill or other. She could never keep all the names straight so she just referred to them as her "vitamins."

CHAPTER 13
NEW YORK

Needing a change, Marilyn moved to New York and enjoyed exploring the art scene. She met Lee Strasberg and was accepted as a new student at the Actor's Studio. It seemed every fascinating person she met introduced her to another fascinating person. She could eat a street vendor hot dog at lunchtime and go to the Met that same evening. Marilyn loved it all. And living in New York meant she'd get the chance to renew her friendship with Arthur Miller.

Arthur Miller had been brought up as the rather pampered son of Augusta and Isiadore, owners of a prominent clothing manufacturing business. When the Wall Street Crash of 1929 happened, the family lost their wealth and Arthur, at age 14, went from being driven by a chauffeur to his family's Manhattan home to living in Brooklyn where he delivered bread in the early morning before school to help support his family.

This bird's eye view of how different the world could be for the Haves and the Have Nots (and how quickly one could go from being one to being the other) made a deep impression on Arthur and would influence him as he rose to prominence as a playwright, winning the Pulitzer Prize in 1949 for his play Death Of A Salesman.

He and Marilyn began having a quiet affair. When the tabloids asked her questions about Miller, Marilyn insisted they were just friends and reminded them he was married.

The FBI began a file on Marilyn at this time.

Miller's success as a writer had been largely due to his wife, Mary Grace Slattery. In addition to giving him two children, her ability and willingness to work long hours, first as a waitress and then as a copy editor, paid the majority of their bills so that Miller could work on his plays.

His wife knew just how human he was but Marilyn gazed up at him like he was a genius. To her friends she compared him to Abraham Lincoln. It's possible he considered her valuable for future inspiration. He had already used his father, mother, and wife as inspiration for his work. It's also possible he liked the idea that she had a great deal of wealth and the potential to earn even more in the future.

If Arthur left his wife, he'd have alimony and child support to pay, but his more immediate concern was paying for legal fees.

When Miller tried to renew his Belgian passport he had been subpoenaed to testify before the House Un-American Activities Committee. Originally formed in 1938, it had been stirred into action by Senator Joseph McCarthy who claimed that over 200 "card carrying" Communists had infiltrated the United States government. When these allegations were proven to be untrue, he switched his focus and pointed his finger at the entertainment world. He claimed it was filled with Communists and Communist sympathizers and that these people might use their talents to sneak anti-American propaganda into the radio shows, television, movies, books, and plays that true blue Americans enjoyed every day.

Over 320 artists suspected of being Communist sympathizers were blacklisted, destroying their reputations and making it impossible for them to find work. Some had their passports taken away while others were threatened with jail if they did not answer any and all questions put before them by the Committee. Evil villain like, this committee offered to go easier on these artists if they were willing to "name names" of peers who might be of interest to the Committee.

Among those artists accused of Communist sympathies were Dashiell Hammett, Waldo Salt, Lillian Hellman, Lena Horne, Paul Robeson, Elia Kazan, Aaron Copland, Leonard Bernstein, Charlie Chaplin, and Arthur Miller.

In a February 12, 1955 broadcast, Walter Winchell told listeners "America's best known blonde moving picture star is now the darling of left-wing intelligentsia, several of whom are listed as Red Fronters." The story had been written by FBI Director J. Edgar Hoover, who had been keeping a file on Arthur Miller since Arthur's college days at the University of Michigan.

Marilyn (who, for a time was seeing both Arthur and her ex-husband Joe) stood firmly by Arthur's side, putting her own reputation and career at risk by doing so.

For the House Un-American Activities Committee (HUAC), Miller was a juicy fish indeed.

From an FBI Office Memorandum dated July 2, 1956:

"Miller was under communist discipline in the 1930s and was a CP member in 1943,1946, and 1947. He has been a member of or connected with a number of CP front organizations. Miller testified before HUAC on 6/21/56, and admitted having attended meetings in 1939 or 1940 which he understood were meetings of CP writers, however Miller refused to furnish any names. Miller also admitted having contributed to communist fronts."

Miller testified about his political leanings but refused to name others, unlike his longtime friend Elia Kazan, who had done so. As Miller stated to the committee: "My conscience will not permit me to use the name of another person."

Rep. Francis Walter (D-Pa.), committee chairman had promised Miller he would not be asked to name names but then did so anyway. Most of the other people forced to testify before the committee invoked the Fifth Amendment protection against self-incrimination but Miller invoked the First Amendment protection of free speech, which Miller cleverly explained must include the freedom to remain silent, and refrain from speech.

Walter Winchell was following this story closely. "Marilyn Monroe's new romance is a long time pro-lefto," he explained to his listeners. It was his job, after all, to keep Americans informed of such things.

Congressman Walter offered Miller a deal. The possibility of contempt charges would be dropped if Marilyn would agree to be photographed shaking hands with Walter. Miller immediately refused.

A congressional vote found Miller in contempt by a vote of 373 to 9.

During the hearing Miller asked for his passport to be returned to him so he could travel to England to see the production of one of his plays and to "be with the woman who will then be my wife." Reporters asked who that might be and Miller told them "I will marry Marilyn Monroe before July 13, when she is scheduled to go to London to make a picture. When she goes to London, she will go as Mrs. Miller."

Many wondered if Miller had learned a thing or two about PR from his bride-to-be.

What Walter Winchell hadn't realized was that Miller's infatuation with Marilyn would be viewed by many as the most understandable and all-American thing he had ever done.

A U.S. Circuit Court of Appeals overturned the contempt of congress conviction, on the grounds that Miller had been misled by Walter.

During this time Marilyn made important changes in her career. To begin with, she became the first woman to ever form her own production company, Marilyn Monroe Enterprises. The next change was firing her drama coach Natasha Lytess.

For years Lytess had stood faithfully by Marilyn's side and in fact insisted on being on set for every scene, frustrating directors and delaying productions. Many felt her teaching had caused Marilyn to ignore her natural instincts and that the greatest contribution of Lytess seemed to have been to teach Marilyn to sound like a sexy cartoon character. Marilyn replaced Lytess with Lee Strasberg's daughter, Paula.

Her next film would be the movie Bus Stop. Although by now Marilyn was a gifted singer, the role required her to sing badly, dance awkwardly, and deliver all her lines in an Ozark-Oklahoma accent.

The result? Her first Golden Globe nomination.

THE ACTORS' STUDIO
SECOND ANNUAL BENEFIT
World Premiere Presentation
TENNESSEE WILLIAMS'
THE ROSE TATTOO
BURT LANCASTER · ANNA MAGNANI
ASTOR THEATRE

THE ROSE TATTOO

THE ROSE TATTOO

CHAPTER 14
MRS. ARTHUR MILLER

On June 29 Marilyn and Arthur were married at the Westchester County Courthouse in White Plains, N.Y. Two days later they had a second ceremony at home. After a two week honeymoon trip they left for London where Marilyn would begin filming The Prince And The Showgirl with Sir Laurence Olivier.

One week into the filming she noticed Arthur had left his notebook lying open on the dining table and Marilyn was devastated by what she read. As she described it to the Strasbergs later, "It was something about how disappointed he was in me, how he thought I was some kind of angel but now he guessed he was wrong—that his first wife had let him down but I had done something worse. Olivier was beginning to think I was a troublesome bitch, and Arthur said he no longer had a decent answer to that one."

Things on the set were no better. Olivier had no patience for The Method and began to ridicule Marilyn on set, implying that he wasn't sure if she could read or count to three. It seemed to her that whenever he had to be around her he acted "like someone slumming." It got no better when his wife, Vivien Leigh--Scarlett O'Hara herself—came to the set and looked down her regal nose at her.

Marilyn never tried to frustrate people on a movie set. She simply had a strong sense of how the average fan would perceive things. She understood that filmgoers sitting in a theatre didn't care one bit how things had gone on set or how many takes had been required. All they'd care about was how great the movie was. In this she was correct.

Mid-filming, Marilyn learned she was pregnant but suffered a miscarriage only a few weeks later, on August 1st.

As she bit her tongue and finished the project (which Olivier later said was wonderful), Bus Stop was released in London to rave reviews. On October 29, Marilyn, along with 20 other actors including Brigitte Bardot, Joan Crawford, Anita Ekberg, and Victor Mature, were presented to the Queen. As Her Majesty stopped in front of her, Marilyn did a perfect curtsy, and felt amazed at how far she had come.

She and Arthur returned home and things were never the same between them. Unlike Joe, he let her choose her own clothes and seemed unbothered by her tendency to look and act as she chose, but she could never forget the words he had written about her.

She began to drink more frequently and, when drunk, would snap at him, sometimes humiliating him in front of guests. When this happened, he would simply fall silent and leave the room.

That fall she began another film, Let's Make Love, with Yves Montand. Marilyn and Arthur became close friends with Yves and his wife, the actress Simone Signoret. Despite this, Marilyn and Yves enjoyed a brief affair. As Yves would later recall, "Simone was very wise. I will not say she closed her eyes, but at least she lowered her lids." The French actress held her head up in public but was devastated, at one point, telephoning Marilyn and sobbing and begging her to leave her husband alone.

Arthur, on the other hand, seemed to have no reaction at all.

By this time Marilyn had gotten used to a cycle of insomnia leading to drug induced sleep and then horribly groggy mornings and day hours feeling lousy, which led to more pills.

For years Marilyn had been doing what is known as 'doctor shopping', seeing numerous doctors in order to obtain prescription medication while not telling them which other meds she was on or whether she had other physicians prescribing for her. This is common behavior for people addicted to prescription medication. Because addiction very much involves the emotions and can affect mood, the addicted person often uses charm or sweetness to obtain such meds and can just as quickly become enraged if the prescriber refuses to give him or her the drugs they so crave.

There are doctors without number who give in to the pressure put on them by the addict and give them what they ask for. They may do this out of greed for the person's money or because they just don't want to put themselves through the experience of telling the addict No.

Marilyn's current psychiatrist, Dr. Marianne Kris, was an idealistic doctor who took her work seriously. She'd been recommended to Marilyn by Sigmund Freud's daughter.. Dr. Kris wanted to help her patient. She was about to learn more about Hollywood than she ever wanted to know.

CHAPTER 15:
EVERYONE LIKED IT HOT

Marilyn continued to crave dramatic roles. Lee Strasberg seemed to feel she had great potential. In his opinion, the finest actor to come out of the Actor's Studio was Marlon Brando and the second greatest was Marilyn Monroe.

It was Strasberg's belief that some actors were "blocked" by events in their past and for these, he made it a requirement that they begin analysis. Brando had taken this advice and had claimed it had helped him tremendously when he was filming A Streetcar Named Desire.

Sensing Marilyn had issues in her past—possibly because she talked about them all the time—Strasberg directed her to begin therapy. Eager to advance in the Actor's Studio, and in the eyes of Strasberg, Marilyn had started seeing a psychiatrist three times a week and then increased that frequency to five times a week.

At one of her sessions Marilyn had commented about having

difficulty sleeping sometimes.

The doctor immediately wrote her a prescription, assuring her if that pill didn't do the trick, there were plenty of others they could try.

She may have wished for a serious role, but her next one was in yet another comedy, Some Like It Hot. She was paired with Tony Curtis and Jack Lemmon, who had taken the role after Jerry Lewis turned it down.*

While agreeing that working with Marilyn could be frustrating at times, such as when she required 59 takes to say the line "Who's got the bourbon?", Lemmon regarded her as a comic genius with naturally perfect timing. Unfortunately for Marilyn, the gifts she had she did not value.

For her role in the movie, Marilyn won a Golden Globe Award for Best Actress In A Comedy.

The week after they finished the film, Marilyn had another miscarriage.

*Lemmon, who would receive an Oscar nomination for the role, sent Jerry Lewis chocolates to say Thank You, and did this every year for the next 47 years, until Lemmon's death in 2005.

CHAPTER 16
THE MISFITS

Arthur decided to make a gift for Marilyn. He'd written a short story in the early days of their courtship and he turned this story, The Misfits, into a screenplay. It would be Marilyn's 29th film and the last she would complete.

What began as a hopeful project quickly turned into a nightmare for everyone involved. Marilyn, who as a young girl had often pretended Clark Gable was her father, was thrilled to be working with him but the tension between Marilyn and Arthur made everyone uncomfortable.

Marilyn was having pills flown in for her every other day and getting injectable drugs from local doctors; she was often overmedicated and had slurred speech and an unsteady walk. Midway through the filming she claimed to be suffering from nervous exhaustion and flew to L.A. to spend a week in a private clinic. After returning to Nevada she often kept her costars waiting in the over 100 degree temperatures while she failed to emerge from her trailer.

Just when things on set seemed as awkward as they could possibly get, Miller began having an affair with on set photographer Inge Morath which he made no effort to conceal from Marilyn or anyone else.

On November 4th filming was completed. Marilyn and Arthur returned home to L.A. on separate flights and Marilyn announced their separation to the press.

The next day Clark Gable had a heart attack and was hospitalized. On November 16th he had a second, massive heart attack and died at age 59.

Marilyn learned of his death when a reporter called her at 4am, asking her how it felt to know she'd killed him. Many people, including Gable's widow (his fifth wife, who was pregnant with the child he'd never see), held Marilyn responsible for his death and this charge is mostly untrue but not entirely so.

Clark Gable had died as a result of his lifestyle choices: he'd smoked three packs of cigarettes a day for 30 years, had recently put himself on a crash diet to regain his former slim build, and despite his age and the desert heat had insisted on doing almost all of his own stunts including being physically dragged by a pickup

truck.

Is it likely all of these things put him at increased risk for the heart attack that killed him? Yes.

Did it help his condition to have to stand around outside in the desert for hours at a time while Marilyn failed to appear on set? No.

It did seem that Marilyn had contributed to his death and when Kay Gable banned her from the funeral it seemed she felt the same way. Marilyn was devastated.

Her doctor, Marianne Kris, felt Marilyn had reached rock bottom. At her suggestion, Marilyn agreed to sign herself in voluntarily to Cornwall University New York Hospital. Marilyn was then immediately transported to the Payne Whitney Clinic, the psychiatric ward of New York Hospital and was placed in a locked room.

Dr. Kris had had Marilyn placed on a psychiatric hold: the proper course of action when a psychiatrist believes the patient to be at imminent risk of harm to self or others. Although Marilyn had voluntarily signed herself in, she could only be released if and when the facility determined she was no longer at risk.

Letter written to Lee and Paula Strasberg, which they received Wednesday, February 8th:

Dear Lee and Paula,

Dr. Kris has put me in the hospital under the care of

Two idiot doctors. I'm locked up with all these poor nutty

People. I'm sure to end up a nut too if I stay in this nightmare.

Please help me. This is the last place I should be.

I love you both.

Marilyn

P.S.

I'm on the dangerous floor. It's like a cell. They had my

bathroom locked and I couldn't get a key to get into it,

so I broke the glass. But outside of that I haven't done

anything that is uncooperative.

Actually Marilyn had yelled for a while and then removed all her clothes and yelled some more. When this had no effect she picked up a chair and broke a window and then, holding a jagged piece of glass in her hand, threatened to use it on the orderlies. She was treated like any other patient: they temporarily placed her in restraints until she calmed down.

On her third day in the hospital a fellow patient loaned her some money for the ward pay phone and after being unable to reach anyone else, she got through to Joe and begged him to come get her out.

That night the hospital staff had a furious ex-ballplayer to deal with. Joe came to the hospital and demanded Marilyn be released

```
        TELEGRAM              Feb.27th


Marilyn Monroe
Nurological Institute Clinic
Presbyterian Hospital
168th & Broadway
New York City, N.Y.

Dear Marilyn:

The best reappraisals are born in the

worst crisis.  It has happened to all

of us in relative degrees.  Be glad

for it and don't be afraid of being

afraid.  It can only help.  Relax and

enjoy it.  I send you my thoughts and

my warmest affections.

Marlon
```

into his care. The staff told him it would have to be approved by Dr. Kris so he called her and said if Marilyn wasn't discharged by the next day he would "take the hospital apart brick by brick."

The next day Marilyn was transferred to an unlocked ward in the Columbia Presbyterian Medical Center. She also fired Dr. Kris. Marlon Brando sent her a telegram that had made her smile and Joe visited her every day. He also did something Marilyn thought was just marvelous: he consulted his attorney and had him draw up papers ensuring no doctor could ever hospitalize Marilyn again without his consent.

After three weeks Marilyn left the hospital and flew to Florida to enjoy a two week vacation with Joe. Many people wondered if they might be planning to remarry but there was soon another man in the picture:

Joe's old pal, Frank Sinatra.

CHAPTER 17:
OLD BLUE EYES

Frank had known Marilyn for years but they began a romance that would last the rest of the year. According to Frank it began when she was a houseguest and he got up in the middle of the night to find Marilyn standing nude in front of the refrigerator, unable to decide between lemonade and orange juice.

In a way, they made a great combination. Marilyn already enjoyed his pals and she loved going to the best restaurants and nightclubs. Frank enjoyed having such a beautiful woman by his side.

His pals, of course, meant The Rat Pack. This group of colorful entertainers was originally led by Humphrey Bogart. One night he arrived home with them and his wife, actress Lauren

Bacall, commented they looked like a pack of rats: the nickname was born.

After Bogart's death the group consisted of Sinatra, Sammy Davis Jr., Dean Martin, Jerry Lewis, Peter Lawford, and Joey Bishop. Part time members of the group were Nat King Cole and Shirley MacClaine.

Like Frank, Marilyn was an admirer of the freshly elected President John F. Kennedy and had met both Jack and his younger brother, Bobby (the newly appointed U.S. Attorney General) at several private dinner parties.

Sometimes Marilyn spent the weekend with Frank at Cal Neva. He'd become the new owner of the luxury Lake Tahoe casino resort earlier in the year (along with silent partner Sam Giancana*). Built in 1928, the resort sat on the border of California and Nevada: hence the name. The slot machines were fitted with wheels on the bottom and in the event of a raid, an alarm would sound and staff with colorful nicknames would wheel the machines over to the "Nevada" side. Frank had added a concert hall and a helipad but had kept much of the grounds as they were. The main building was surrounded by several finely built cabins, each one with a wraparound deck and breathtaking view of pine trees that seemed to stretch on forever.

*Giancana was rumored to be a high ranking figure in the world of organized crime.

Beneath the resort was a series of tunnels: some led to discreet exits, for guests who might want extra privacy when arriving or leaving, and other tunnels led into neighboring casinos. Designed during Prohibition, these tunnels had been originally used to smuggle alcohol in and out of the resort. There was also a tunnel which connected the owner's cabin to the cabin next to his, connected via the secret trap door in the cabin's bedroom closet. It was a popular getaway spot and in fact had been a place Jack and Bobby's parents had taken them when they were children.

Marilyn was able to meet Ella Fitzgerald, the singer whose records she had listened to, to find out what fine singing sounded like. Marilyn was upset to learn how black entertainers were often unable to work at many nightclubs and that even when they were, they often weren't allowed to use the same backstage facilities as white performers. Sammy Davis Jr. spoke of having to use the men's room to change between numbers because he wasn't allowed to use the regular dressing room. Ella told her when police caught black performers backstage, they'd arrest them and then ask them for their autographs afterward.

Troubled by these stories, Marilyn called the owner of The Mocambo and made him an offer: if he booked Ella Fitzgerald, Marilyn would come and sit in the front row every night. He agreed and when Ella sang at The Mocambo, to rave reviews, it helped open the door for black entertainers to work and be treated well in places that had previously shut them out.

By the end of the year, Frank was beginning to be concerned that Marilyn might be bad for his image. He had considered marrying her, but the pills were a dealbreaker.

As things cooled between them, Marilyn spent more time with Joe. At Christmas he surprised her by decorating her apartment with a tree and what she called "a forestful of poinsettias."

And then the new year began. Kay Gable invited Marilyn to the christening of her baby boy, John Clark, and Marilyn felt somewhat forgiven.

Her divorce from Arthur became final and Marilyn made a statement to the press:

"Mr. Miller is a wonderful man and a great writer, but
it didn't work out that we should be husband and wife.
But everybody I ever loved, I still love a little."

CHAPTER 18
BAD MEDICINE

Marilyn purchased a home in Brentwood, a charming Spanish style hacienda next to Pat and Peter Lawford. At the entry to the home was a curious engraved tile that told visitors CURSUM PERFICIO. This Latin motto, translated, means "My journey is over."

She became friends with her neighbors. Peter, a minor film star, had been discovered for his looks while working as a theatre usher and had married Patricia Kennedy, daughter of the powerful Kennedy clan.

Pat especially liked that Marilyn found Peter "creepy," and had shot him down when he'd met her years earlier. No affair would ever end their friendship.

Pat had been raised with flexible standards for male fidelity. Her father Joe had advised his sons to "get laid as often as possible," and her mother, Rose, had a gift for looking the other way.

As a wife herself Pat was willing to look the other way when her husband had one fling after the other, only objecting if the girl of the moment tried to telephone their home.

It delighted Pat to hold dinner parties and to seat her brother, John, between two equally beautiful women (usually actresses) and watch him be unable to decide which one to pay attention to.

They knew John regarded Marilyn as a favorite. It was rumored they'd had a brief affair while both had been houseguests at Bing Crosby's a few months earlier. Peter was planning a birthday gala for John, to be held at Madison Square Garden on May 19, and he asked Marilyn if she'd like to be the one to sing Happy Birthday to him. Marilyn loved the idea and began deciding what kind of dress she'd like to wear.

It was a pleasant diversion that took her mind off the problem of her housekeeper, Eunice Murray. She'd been hired by Dr. Greenson and had become quite an irritation. In fact, Marilyn had fired her that spring only to have Mrs. Murray return to work the next day as if nothing had happened. It seemed easier at the time to just let her stay.

In addition to cooking and cleaning, Mrs. Murray always seemed to be eavesdropping whenever Marilyn had a friend over or when she was on the phone. She would often catch Mrs. Murray on the phone to Dr. Greenson, seeming to be telling him what she had just seen or heard.

And there was more: this housekeeper felt the need to tell Marilyn and her friends where they should shop and what they should buy. If they didn't take her suggestions, she'd act insulted and would cluck her tongue in disapproval. Each time Marilyn purchased items and furniture for her new home without consulting Mrs. Murray, the housekeeper became insulted.

Marilyn was being treated by two doctors at this time: her psychiatrist, Dr. Ralph Greenson, and her internist, Dr. Hyman Engelberg, and neither of them had maintained the proper doctor-patient distance which is essential for good care.

Anyone looking through Marilyn's address book would see the names and numbers of no less than 36 doctors and dozens of RNs. This was no surprise to her doctors; they knew of her doctor shopping and for some reason, continued to prescribe for Marilyn anyway.

Dr. Greenson had seemed to be making up new doctor-patient protocol as he saw fit. He regularly invited her to his home for dinner with his family, or for drinks in his living room. He seemed to believe Marilyn needed to be seen at least five times a week, sometimes seven, and often he and Marilyn would end their therapy session by sharing a bottle of wine.

He decided it would be wise to have someone living in Marilyn's home who could be his eyes and ears and report back to him about anything of concern.

Dr. Greenson advised Marilyn he thought this was a good idea and so she had agreed. If Greenson was seriously worried about her stability and thought her an imminent risk, he could have had her placed in a lockdown facility were it not for the well-intended interference of Joe DiMaggio.

Since Joe still seemed so attached to Marilyn, would he have listened if a doctor sat him down and explained exactly why a hospitalization was needed? Would he have consented if he believed that failing to do this might result in her death? Absolutely. But Dr. Greenson never attempted to do this. It's possible he himself was no longer capable of accurately assessing Marilyn's condition.

Instead of placing a medical worker in her home, Dr. Greenson had Marilyn hire Eunice Murray to be her housekeeper. Murray had no medical training whatsoever and in fact was a high school dropout, but Greenson owed her a favor and so she got the job.

CHAPTER 19
GALA

Marilyn and Dean Marin began working on a film called Something's Got To Give and soon she had many of her old problems: she was late to the set or absent altogether. She also insisted all the other actresses in the film get their hair dyed a darker shade to ensure she'd be the only blonde. Even the brunettes had to get their hair dyed a darker shade of brown.

Marilyn had taken many sick days and executives at Twentieth Century Fox weren't pleased when, during one of her sick episodes, she was suddenly on their TV sets, at the president's Birthday Gala.

Over 15,000 people had turned out for the celebration, each paying between $100-$1000 per ticket for an event that doubled as a fundraiser to pay off the Democratic National Committee's deficit from JFK's campaign.

Comedian Jack Benny was the emcee and the performers

included all of Kennedy's favorites: Ella Fitzgerald, Jimmy Durante, Peggy Lee, Henry Fonda, Maria Callas, Harry Belafonte, Peter Lawford, Mike Nichols, Elaine May, and Marilyn.

She wore a dress described as "skin and beads" that somehow made her look nude and dressed at the same time. Marilyn took the stage and sang "Happy Birthday Mr. President" in her trademark sexy voice and JFK thanked her, stating, "…I can now retire after having had Happy Birthday sung to me in such a sweet and wholesome way."

Back in L.A., filming continued. One night scene involved Marilyn skinny dipping in a swimming pool while wearing a nude colored bodystocking. Marilyn, always mindful of PR, had an idea: she removed the bodystocking and had them film the scene with her nude. Since the only part of her that would be seen in the film would be her face and one ankle, lifted up onto the pool's edge, it made no actual difference what she wore.

Marilyn knew the difference would be the shocking headlines it would inspire, which would then make everyone want to see the movie.

Fox executives had a different idea. They informed her she'd been absent 12 out of 34 days, too sick to work but well enough to sing to John F. Kennedy. They fired Marilyn from the picture.

Her costar, Dean Martin, flatly refused to work with any actress but Marilyn. He reminded them his contract stipulated he had final approval of all his leading ladies.

WESTERN COSTUME CO.
5335 Melrose Ave.
HOLLYWOOD 38, CALIF.   HOllywood 9-1451

THEATRICAL COSTUMES · PROPERTIES · EQUIPMENT · WIGS AND HAIR GOODS · COSTUME JEWELRY

ORIGINAL INVOICE

Invoice No. 69778

700   DATE 5/24/62

TO.   Miss Marilyn Monroe
       12305 Firth Helena Dr.
       Los Angeles 49, Calif.

TERMS: NET 10 DAYS E.O.M.

SHIPPING SHEET NO.	QUAN.		UNIT PRICE	TOTAL
82692	1	Made to Order Dress		
		Labor and Material including necessary Overtime		1,027.36
		Cost of Rhinestones & Mirrors (not including the actual beading)		321.89
	1	Pr. Shoes		35.68
				1,384.93
		Sales Tax		55.40
				1,440.33
		Less Deposit		300.00
dw		PURCHASE	Balance Due	1,140.33

The foregoing articles are rented from Western Costume Co. upon the terms set forth in the shipping sheet Envelope signed by the representative of the lessee to which shipping sheet reference is hereby made.

The public was also upset, mainly because it meant they'd never get to see that swimming scene.

That July, waiting for Fox's decision, Marilyn spent a lot of time with Joe. They rode bicycles and shared dinners and she took him along when she bought clothes so she could model for him and he could tell her how lovely she was.

She enjoyed the process of decorating the house and had ordered many items from Mexico, delighting when each one arrived. Still, she was worried. The studio was taking a long time to come to its senses.

In the last weekend of July Marilyn accompanied Pat and Peter to Cal Neva. On the flight over, she drank heavily and then refused to leave the plane after it landed. The flight crew had to carry her off the plane and into the waiting car.

When Frank saw her, he was horrified. He got her settled in the cabin beside his and then immediately telephoned Dr. Greenson, asking him just what kind of treatment he was giving her.

Marilyn was continuously tipsy that night and much of the next day. The only person who didn't seem to notice she was in bad shape was Marilyn herself.

Peter, Pat, and Frank watched as Marilyn rummaged through her purse, pulling out numerous syringes and bottles of pills and began using a safety pin to pierce the end of each capsule before swallowing it. It was a technique that could have caused immediate death but Marilyn had done this trick for so long, she thought it was harmless. Seeing their shocked expressions, she explained, "It makes them work faster."

Frank left the room. Few things scared Sinatra but drugs terrified him. He'd lost count of how many pills she had taken and had no idea what they even were. He went directly to the car valet, who knew from one look at his boss that something was very wrong.

"Get her out of here and get her out of here now," Sinatra ordered.

The valet nodded. Marilyn was whisked back to L.A. in record time and nobody asked any questions.

Back home, Marilyn was a little embarrassed. She should have known better than to drink; she had no head for alcohol

Her mood lifted when she learned Fox was rehiring her and adding a nice raise to sweeten the deal. Not that she needed the money; she'd just gotten an offer from an Italian film company for a four film deal worth 10 million. Money would never be a problem again.

Even more exciting, she was going to be playing Jean Harlow in a film about her life. Sidney Skolsky had gone with her to meet Harlow's mother, "Mama Jean" Bello, and had gotten her full approval to do the film.

Everything, it seemed, was looking up. Marilyn planned to reward herself with a lazy weekend at home.

CHAPTER 20
CLOSING SCENES

Friday will be a mostly uneventful day: Marilyn will go to a local nursery to purchase plants for her backyard and then will stop at a pharmacy to pick up her prescription for chloral hydrate.

Her friend and publicist, Pat Newcomb, will stay for dinner and will spend the night. It's a kind of joke between them, that Marilyn is jealous of how well Pat sleeps. In fact Pat will sleep in until 10am Saturday and Marilyn will be irritated by that fact. In her opinion, sleeping soundly all night is one thing but sleeping until 10am is just showing off. This will make Pat laugh and Marilyn will laugh too.

That Saturday, August 4, will be Mrs. Murray's last working day. She'd requested time off for a vacation and Marilyn told her it would be fine and not to come back. It's likely there's a bit of tension about this: Marilyn looking forward to living alone without being spied on and Mrs. Murray, maybe feeling unappreciated. She will plan to stay the night and then leave on Sunday morning.

Marilyn's medication plan has been changed somewhat. Rather than taking one large dose at bedtime, Dr. Greenson has Marilyn taking several doses throughout the day. These doses will accumulate in her body so that by bedtime she'll be groggy enough to sleep. At least that will be the plan.

During that Saturday Marilyn will speak by phone to several friends and has tentative plans to have dinner at the Lawford's. By late afternoon she will decide not to go, although Peter will call her several times, encouraging her to change her mind.

At 4:30pm Dr. Greenson will arrive for their regular appointment which will last an hour and a half. It will seem to be uneventful as Dr. Greenson knows Mrs. Murray is getting ready to move out and he will not seem concerned about Marilyn living alone. He will leave at 6pm and will drive the one mile home to his family and will have dinner.

Marilyn will putter around, talking on the phone to friends, and will have a nice conversation with Joe's son, Joe Jr., from 7:15pm-7:30pm. He will prove to be one of the only reliable witnesses from this point forward. According to Joe Jr., she sounded great. Her speech wasn't slurred and she sounded happy to hear he'd ended things with his current girlfriend. Joe Jr. will say he felt better after talking to her and Mrs. Murray will state Marilyn was smiling after talking to the young man.

Marilyn will tell Mrs. Murray she's going to bed just after 8pm. This will be fine by Mrs. Murray because she's a Perry Mason fan and plans to watch a two year old rerun that will begin at 8:30pm.

Peter Lawford will report he spoke to Marilyn on the phone sometime between 8:30pm and 8:50pm and will admit he had had several drinks by this time. Still, he'll insist Marilyn's speech sounded somewhat slurred and this made him concerned. Lawford will call his agent, Milton Ebbins, who will advise him against going to Marilyn's home to check on her.

Ebbins will call Marilyn's attorney, Milton Rudin, and Rudin will call Marilyn's home at 9pm. Eunice Murray will answer the phone and, without checking on Marilyn, will tell him she's fine and then will hang up the phone. It's likely the 9pm call will bother her, as it will interrupt her program.

Marilyn will make a few more phone calls but between the hours of 8:30pm and 10pm we do not have the records because in the early morning hours of Sunday the FBI will seize Marilyn's phone records, upon the direct order of J. Edgar Hoover. This could only have been done under a direct request from either Attorney General Robert Kennedy or from President John F. Kennedy.

Marlon Brando will state Marilyn called him and that they had a brief conversation. He will flatly refuse to elaborate.

Sometime between 9pm and 10pm Marilyn will take the fatal dose of chloral hydrate. The amount she takes will be only slightly higher than the amount to which she's become accustomed. It will kill her but it will just barely kill her.

She has a habit, when already groggy from medication, of being unable to remember whether she'd taken the last dose or not and erring on the side of recklessness. It is almost certain that is what happened on her final night.

The last dose will kill her instantly. In her final moments Marilyn will not have fear or pain.

At 10pm the Perry Mason movie will end and Mrs. Murray will check on Marilyn. Worried, she'll call Dr. Greenson, who will arrive minutes later.

Dr. Greenson will be joined by Dr. Engelberg and neither will be able to revive Marilyn. At 10:30pm Dr. Greenson will call Marilyn's lawyer Milton Rudin and at 10:45pm Rudin will phone in a message to be delivered to Marilyn's press agent, Arthur Jacobs, who is at the Henry Mancini concert at the Hollywood Bowl.

At 10:45pm Jacobs will tell his fiancé, who is beside him, that Marilyn has just died. The two of them will leave. He'll drop her off at home and will proceed to Marilyn's, arriving about 11:15pm.

An ambulance will arrive at the house around midnight and will leave almost immediately afterward. California ambulances were prohibited from transporting dead bodies.

At 4:25am Dr. Greenson will call the police, to notify them of Marilyn's death.

CHAPTER 21
THE SEARCH FOR VILLAINS

In the case of Marilyn Monroe there has been endless speculation, most of it in the form of juicy gossip to sell magazines. Much of the gossip has involved whether or not the Mafia had anything to do with Marilyn's death, whether the Kennedy family had anything to do with her death, or a combination of the two.

These rumors are false.

Marilyn knew, and occasionally dated, a few people rumored to be involved with the Mafia but it's absolutely unlikely she ever had any information about their activities. The Mafia has always been built on secrecy, and it was no different in 1962. Even the wives of alleged mobsters had no idea what their husbands did. Certainly their girlfriends would not have been any wiser. No one could survive in the world of the Mafia if they ran around blabbing their business to sexy blondes. The Mafia would have had no interest in harming Marilyn and in fact would have treated her with extra kid gloves because she was known to be DiMaggio's girl.

It has been suggested Marilyn kept a diary, and she did. Robert Kennedy had teased her that she often forgot some of the clever things he said and he suggested she keep a diary. Since both John F. Kennedy and Robert Kennedy were, as the President and Attorney General, quite well versed in politics, it's unlikely either of them ever shared any sort of secrets with Marilyn or any information more detailed than the type they'd give to any journalist. Whatever was in Marilyn's diary was harmless.

The autopsy would reveal she had died at age 36 of an overdose of nembutal and chloral hydrate and that her stomach showed no trace of these drugs.

The diary, whatever it contained, was reportedly given to the coroner's office, although it was never seen by Dr. Thomas Naguchi, who performed the autopsy. He has stated he took many organ and tissue samples and that the next day these samples and the rumored diary were gone. As his staff would later tell him, they had believed the investigation was closed.

It's unknown whether the Kennedy family or anyone working for them had anything to do with these events, although it's likely the Kennedys would have wanted to distance themselves from the scandal as much as possible.

At the time of the autopsy, Dr. Naguchi ruled Marilyn's death a probable suicide, based on the large amount of drugs Marilyn had in her system and the information that was available to him at that time.

The only coverup seemed to be of two varieties: medical professionals lying to protect their professional reputations and people covering up the specific details of Marilyn's death to present a better image for her fans. These two coverups took place at once, with many persons being aware of the lies on both sides.

Her psychiatrist had been unethical in his treatment for some time and had been prescribing in an unethical way. Her internist had also been prescribing haphazardly and both of them were well aware their patient was an addict at risk of overdose. Both of them knew she required inpatient treatment, not for any kind of mental illness and not for depression, but to wean herself off the drugs and safely go through the withdrawal process. It's likely both of them enjoyed the status of being involved with a star and enjoyed the money they made from her and from her addiction.

When Marilyn was discovered, it was too late to save her life. And it's likely that when they found her, she was a mess. In part to cover themselves and in part to do what they probably thought she would have wanted, they changed the scene. They tried to make her go out like a goddess, not like an addict.

We know she didn't swallow the pills and yet had the drugs in her system. She either used a surgical needle and injected herself, dying instantly, in which case she would have been found with the needle still in her arm, or she administered the drugs using an enema and died instantly, with the apparatus still sticking into her body.

Marilyn owned the equipment and had long been proficient with both methods. We may never know which method was used. Any puncture from a surgical needle would have disappeared within hours and become undetectable in the autopsy, and no further tests could be done on the samples to determine if an enema had been used because the samples were, for whatever reason, thrown away. We do know that the scene would have told the story: a junkie-type death or a grotesque one.

She was a bigger star than that. Maybe that's what they told themselves. We can't let them talk about this in the papers. Maybe that's what they said.

We do know that the first policeman on the scene found her lying face down with her arms straight at the sides, soldier style. It was opinion the body had been moved and it was extremely unlikely anyone would die in that position. He found the body was lying on freshly changed sheets and that the housekeeper had one load of sheets in the dryer and another load in the washer at 4:30am.

Likely the sheets Marilyn had died on.

We know that her psychiatrist and the housekeeper both changed their stories several times and presented a very dramatic story full of holes. Mrs. Murray would claim she had noticed a light still on beneath Marilyn's door. When informed the carpeting was new and so thick that no light from beneath the door could be seen, she changed her story. She had just had a feeling, and she had found the door locked. Except the door was unlocked. Marilyn had a firm rule about never locking that door. Mrs. Murray would then claim she had gone outside and seen through a crack in the curtains that Marilyn was lying in bed. She would revise this to say she had used a fireplace poker to part the curtains. In fact Marilyn kept one solid sheet of fabric covering the entire wall with the window. There was no "part" in this fabric, and when the police arrived it had been completely taken down and folded up into a neat square on a side table.

Her doctor would claim he had to use a fireplace poker (yes, the same one) to break a side window so that he could climb into the room. This story seems unlikely as the police noticed the broken glass was outside the window, not inside. A person standing outside breaking a window would cause glass to be inside, on the floor.

When told she must have swallowed the pills, the police had immediate doubt. There was no glass in the room that could have held liquid to swallow anything. In fact the bathroom attached to the room had no running water. Marilyn had been having the bathroom remodeled and the water had been shut off for over 24 hours. How had she swallowed the pills? Where was the glass? Even more disturbing to the policemen at the scene was that within 15 minutes of voicing these questions, suddenly someone produced a glass lying next to the bed which had not been there before.

After her body was removed, police allowed a throng of press into the room where they trampled over and photographed everything, effectively contaminating the crime scene. After about ten minutes of this the police sealed off the house.

Eunice Murray officially changed her version five separate times and then the police stopped asking her questions. She was allowed to leave the country one week later to travel to Europe and was never questioned by police again. In 1975 she penned a book giving her once again altered version of events but her book begins with her sentence: "I wouldn't take my word for it."

One by one, the people who loved her will get the news. Joe will be notified and will catch the first flight to L.A. United Airlines will hold the flight for him and he'll sit, silently, throughout the trip. Later, at the morgue, he'll be led into a room and when he sees her, he'll scream.

Frank, who had planned to have dinner with Marilyn Sunday night, will be inconsolable.

Berniece will begin the long trip from Tennessee. To her, Marilyn wasn't a star; she was her sister. She will remind herself to be strong for Joe.

In a choked voice, Joe will call Whitey Snyder and will ask him to help. He won't have to say the words; Snyder will know what he needs. He'll arrive at the funeral home with a makeup case and a flask of gin to keep the promise he made. By morning the flask is empty and Marilyn is beautiful again.

The night before the service, Joe will sit beside her casket: praying, sobbing, and talking to his girl.

Flights will be booked as her many friends traveled toward the scene they'd hoped would never happen. Outfits will be chosen. Rides will be arranged. No one will know what to say.

CHAPTER 22
FINAL SCENE

Joe will ban everyone from Hollywood from attending the funeral and will be quoted as saying "If not for her 'friends', she'd still be here." Frank Sinatra, Dean Martin, Sammy Davis Jr., Peter Lawford, Ella Fitzgerald, they will be left standing at the gate, unable to enter.

Joe will also specifically advise the funeral home staff to keep out "those Goddamned Kennedys," not that either of them tried to attend.

Eunice Murray and Dr. Greenson will be allowed in. Joe will invite Arthur Miller and James Dougherty but both men will choose to stay away.

The press, as always, will be hungry for the story, which now will be her last story. There will be a private service inside for a group of 25 people and when the pallbearers (one of them, her makeup artist, Whitey Snyder) carry the coffin out of the chapel there will be photographers standing on the roof to capture the shot. In these most private moments we can see them, crouched like monkeys, just doing their jobs.

Per Joe's instructions, Judy Garland's voice will fill the chapel with her song, "Somewhere Over The Rainbow," which had been a favorite of Marilyn's ever since that day she saw The Wizard Of Oz and had been so amazed she couldn't leave her seat.

Joe will cry throughout the service.

He will walk behind the pallbearers with tears running down his face. They will lift the lid of the coffin so mourners can say a last goodbye. Joe will lean down for a last kiss and will say "I love you, I love you, I love you."

The coffin will be inserted into a wall crypt as thousands of flashbulbs pop, marking this moment in history.

Keeping the promise he made to Marilyn years earlier, Joe will have red roses delivered to her crypt every week. The order he places at Parisian Florist will read "six fresh long stemmed red roses, three times a week…forever."

Millions of fans will visit Marilyn's crypt and cemetery staff will have to periodically replace the marble facing because it will be stained over and over with red lipstick kisses from fans. Only a few feet away from where Marilyn is interred will be the grave of her friend Natalie Wood. She will die in 1981 of drowning, another

mysterious Hollywood death that will go unsolved. A few feet further down, Peter Lawford's remains will be buried. He will die at age 69. Also in this cemetery rests Marilyn's grandmother, Della, that lady who loved to dance and loved men. Here also will be Ana Lower, the foster mother who rocked Marilyn back and forth when the teasing at school had made the young girl cry.

The FBI will spend over 40 years following Frank Sinatra only to be terrifically disappointed. Other than seducing a married woman and being part of that Wrong Door Raid with DiMaggio, Sinatra was clean. Or lucky.

Joe DiMaggio will never remarry. He will become known to America as Mr. Coffee, the product he will endorse for years.

Arthur Miller stayed married to Inge Morath and they had two children. Later he will write a book about Marilyn which will strongly suggest he placed blame on the Kennedy family. He will later admit he exaggerated the Kennedy angle because he was short on money and needed the book to sell.

In the hallway of the Los Angeles Orphan Home Society (long since renamed Hollygrove), which will remain an orphanage until 2005 and then will be converted into a drug and alcohol treatment facility for youth, there will be a large frame containing photos of Marilyn as a child and as an adult and a plaque describing how the facility's most famous resident went on to become the biggest star in the world. This framed piece will be intended to inspire the hundreds of thousands of children who will pass through, and surely it has.

In Florida state there will be a woman named Gladys Baker Inge, longtime resident of Gainesville. She will occasionally ride her motorized scooter through town to get fresh air but most of the time will be inside. She will live to age 81 and for the last ten years of her life will have no recollection of who Norma Jeane was or if she'd ever known her.

THE END

FILMOGRAPHY
listed by year of release

1948   SCUDDA HOO! SCUDDA HAY!
1948   DANGEROUS YEARS
1949   LADIES OF THE CHORUS
1949   LOVE HAPPY
1950   A TICKET TO TOMAHAWK
1950   THE ASPHALT JUNGLE
1950   RIGHT CROSS
1950   THE FIREBALL
1950   ALL ABOUT EVE
1951   HOMETOWN STORY
1951   AS YOUNG AS YOU FEEL
1951   LOVE NEST
1951   LET'S MAKE IT LEGAL
1952   CLASH BY NIGHT
1952   WE'RE NOT MARRIED
1952   O. HENRY'S FULL HOUSE
1952   MONKEY BUSINESS
1952   DON'T BOTHER TO KNOCK
1953   NIAGRA
1953   GENTLEMEN PREFER BLONDES
1953   HOW TO MARRY A MILLIONAIRE
1954   RIVER OF NO RETURN
1954   THERE'S NO BUSINESS LIKE SHOW BUSINESS
1955   THE SEVEN YEAR ITCH
1956   BUS STOP
1957   THE PRINCE AND THE SHOWGIRL
1959   SOME LIKE IT HOT
1960   LET'S MAKE LOVE
1961   THE MISFITS
1962   SOMETHING'S GOT TO GIVE (unreleased)

PHOTO CREDITS
Listed as they appear in the book

Grace McKee and Gladys Baker, photographer unknown

Gladys and Norma Jeane, photographer unknown

Norma Jeane studio portrait, photographer unknown

Jim Dougherty and Norma Jeane, photographer unknown

Norma Jeane at Radioplane by Jim Conover

Norma Jeane as model by Andre de Dienes

Marilyn and Shelley Winters, by David Sutton

Joe and Marilyn by Milton H. Greene

Marilyn in Korea by Milton H. Greene

Joe and Mariyn by Alfred Eisenstaedt

Joe and Frank Sinatra by Milton H.Greene

Marilyn in pink dress by Philippe Halsman

Marilyn by Alred Eisenstaedt

Betty Grable, Lauren Bacall, and Marilyn, photographer unknown

Marilyn on beach by Andre de Dienes

Marlon Brando and Marilyn by Milton H. Greene

Marilyn and car by Alfred Eisenstaedt

Dean Martin, Jerry Lewis and Marilyn by Joseph Scherer

Marilyn and Arthur Miller by Milton H. Greene

Clark Gable and Marilyn by Milton H. Greene

Marilyn by Alfred Eisenstaedt

Joe at funeral by Lawrence Schiller

MARILYN MONROE
1926 — 1962

BIBLIOGRAPHY

Freedom Of Information And Privacy Acts, Subject: Marilyn Monroe Main File, Federal Bureau of Investigation

Hearings Before The Committee Of Un-American Activities, House of Representatives, Eighty-Fourth Congress, Second Session June 14 and 21, 1956: Investigation Of The Unauthorized Use Of United States Passports—Part 4

Sexual Behavior In The Human Female, Alfred C. Kinsey
copyright 1953, Saunders

Shelley: Also Known As Shirley, Shelley Winters
copyright 1980, Morrow

Frank: The Voice, James Kaplan
copyright 2011, Anchor

The Secret Life Of Marilyn Monroe, J. Randy Taraborrelli
copyright 2009, GrandCentral Publishing

Marilyn Monroe: The Biography, Donald Spoto
copyright 2014, Dansker Press

The Murder of Marilyn Monroe: Case Closed, Jay Margolis
copyright 2014, Skyhorse Publishing

Marilyn: Norma Jeane, Gloria Steinem
copyright 2013, Open Road Media

Goddess: The Secret Lives of Marilyn Monroe, Anthony Summers
copyright 2002, Open Road Media

Timebends: A Life, Arthur Miller
copyright 2013, Grove Press

Arthur Miller, Christopher Bigsby
copyright 2010, Harvard University Press

Marilyn: The Last Months, Eunice Murray
copyright 1975, Pyramid Books

Joe DiMaggio: The Hero's Life, Richard Ben Cramer
copyright 2011, Simon & Schuster

Crypt 33: The Saga of Marilyn Monroe: The Final Word, Adela
Gregory copyright 2012, Citadel

My Sister Marilyn: A Memoir of Marilyn Monroe, Berniece Miracle
copyright 2012, iUniverse

To Norma Jeane, With Love, Jimmie, Jim Dougherty
copyright 2000, BeachHouse Books

Joe and Marilyn: Legends In Love, C. David Heymann
copyright 2014, Atria/Emily Bestler Books

Marilyn Monroe, Maurice Zolotow
copyright 1990, Harpercollins

Coroner, Thomas T. Noguchi, M.D, with Joseph DiMona
copyright 2014, Open Road Media